FOSTERING LOVE

FOSTERING LOVE

One Foster Parent's Journey

Dr. John DeGarmo

CROSSBOOKS
PUBLISHING

CrossBooks™
A Division of LifeWay
1663 Liberty Drive
Bloomington, IN 47403
www.crossbooks.com
Phone: 1-866-879-0502

First published by CrossBooks 5/24/2012

ISBN: 978-1-4627-1854-2 (sc)
ISBN: 978-1-4627-1855-9 (e)

Printed in the United States of America

For Jessica, where ever she might be; and for Daniela, whose inner drive to succeed is inspiring.

"For I was hungry, and you gave me something to eat; I was thirsty, and you gave me something to drink; I was a stranger, and you took me in."

Matthew 25:35

I would like to thank my wife for her unwavering support and patience as I wrote this book. I would also thank my own dear children for being remarkable foster siblings. Finally, I thank Kathy, who took time to read through this book and gave valuable insight.

CHAPTER 1

The call came while I was at work. After much training, a great deal of prayer, and a large amount of waiting, our house was finally set to have a foster child come live with us. In fact, we weren't just getting one foster child, we were getting two; two little girls. I was nervous, confused, and anxious. How would they act in our house? Why were they in foster care? How long would they stay with us? Many questions flew through my head as we prepared our hearts, and our home, for them.

Our own children were excited, as well, though for different reasons. They were excited to have two new sisters come live with them. Kelly, my Australian wife of nine years, and I were certainly depending on them to help in little ways. Ways like helping to keep the house clean, help feed the new additions to our home, and most importantly, help love these hurting children. We had moved into our new house only a few months beforehand, and already we had to reshuffle some rooms around. Our two daughters, Kolby (aged six) and Jace (aged five) both had their own separate rooms. Our son, Brody (aged three) had the largest room upstairs, let alone the entire house. The room is a long one, stretching from one side of the house to the other, though it is a narrow one, with a slanted ceiling.

"He will have to share his room with the oldest girl," said my wife, her bright smile radiating from her petite figure. Her brown hair had recently been cut short, making her ever more beautiful than ever before.

"Yeah, you're right," I replied. "I'll have to put another bed up there." Ken and Cathy, friends of ours from church, had donated an old single bed, so we decided to place the older girl in it, on one side of the room. Brody would sleep on the other side, in a small toddler's bed. The other foster child, a baby, would sleep in a crib in our bedroom, on the main floor.

I hung the phone up, said a silent prayer, and went back to work. It was my sixth year as an English and Drama teacher at the local high school in Eatonton, Georgia, a forty five minute drive from our house in Monticello, a tiny rural town an hour south of Atlanta, and an hour north of Macon. Kelly had recently opened up her own business as a massage therapist, in our fair town of 2,000 residents. As I expected, her charm, her warmth, and her many gifts, given by God, made her an instant success in her business, and her schedule was always full. After all, everyone in the small town knew "Kelly from Australia," and we were very blessed that her career and business was as successful as it was. Indeed, her income was essential to us.

I arrived home and gave Kelly and each of the kids a kiss and hug. Kolby and Jace were at the table, having a snack, and Brody was playing in the lounge room. "Kids, come here," I said, "we have something to talk to you about."

Kelly and I sat across from them in the lounge room. "Children, you know how mommy and I decided to help out other children in need, and you know how we told you we would be foster parents? Well, two little girls are coming to stay with us for awhile."

"Hooray!" Their reaction was immediate, as they jumped off the couch, whooping and hollering. "What time are they coming? Jace asked between missing teeth.

"What's their names?" was Kolby's question. She was excited to be an older sister to even more siblings.

"Where are they going to sleep" Brody wanted to know. His gentle and caring young nature had him concerned for all who were in need.

"Well, one little girl is four, and the other is six months," Kelly told them. "We don't know their names yet. Brody, the four year old is going to sleep at the other end of your room. How does that sound, son?"

"Okay, Mommy," my three year old boy replied.

At church that Wednesday night, our church family was quite interested, as well as supportive. So many questions were flying at us, and we had no answers. The only thing that DFCS, or The Department of Family and Children Services, could tell us is that it would be sometime tonight when they would come. As we were to find out many more times later, as many more foster children would pass through our house, it is often a guessing game when it comes to foster children and DFCS.

It was 10:30, and our own kids had long gone to sleep, when the caseworker arrived with the two girls. The girls were scared, both of them; and why not? They had been taken from their home late at night, taken away from their mother, and placed in a strange home with strange people now looking at them.

The caseworker, Linda, sat across the table from us, sipping a cappuccino I had made for her. "Sarah is four, and Mary Sue is six months," Linda said. "They suffer from poor nutrition and neglect."

"Why were they taken from their homes?" I wanted to know.

"Well," Linda began, "their mother and father were homeless, and moving from one hotel to another. There was also an incident with a knife, and the children were left in a hotel by themselves for awhile, while the parents were out."

"Is the father the father of both children? They look nothing alike," I wanted to know.

"No, there are two different dads. The mother lives with Mary Sue's father, and Sarah's father is in jail," Linda said.

"Is this all the clothes they have?" Kelly asked, pointing to the black plastic bag Linda brought with her.

"Yes, it's not much, but it is all I could get. We had to go into the house with a police escort, as the mother was trying to prevent us from removing the children. If you buy the children new clothes, just keep the receipts and put them with your monthly invoice, and you will be reimbursed."

"How about formula and diapers for Mary Sue?" I asked. "Will we be reimbursed for that too? Diapers are quite expensive.

"Yes. Same as the clothes; just keep the receipts and hand them in with the invoice, too."

It had been a long night, and everyone was tired. We signed the necessary paperwork for taking the two girls into our house that DFCS required, and thanked Linda for everything she had done. But, if Kelly and I thought we were about to go to bed, we were seriously mistaken. It was at this point that the screaming started; screaming that we came to recognize in the future as quite normal for a first night placement into a foster home for a young, confused child. Yet, the screaming was just the beginning.

"I want my mommy! You can't keep me here! I want my mommy!" Sarah screamed, hysterically, as tears flowed down her face. What we were not prepared for came next, very quickly. Sarah ran to the closest door and tried to open it. "You can't keep me here," she screamed again, desperately trying to get out. Holding Mary Sue, I hurried to close the door, while Kelly tried to comfort Sarah.

"I know, I know, Sarah," Kelly said. "I'm so sorry, sweetheart."

Without missing a beat, Sarah ran straight to another door, and tried the same thing. I felt my heart breaking for her. Sarah was simply scared. She didn't know who Kelly and I were. She only knew that she was not home with her mother. As I ran to lock all the doors in the house, Kelly swallowed Sarah up in her arms, and tried to console her with soft kind words. Mary Sue was crying, as well, and was quickly given a bottle. As I was bathing her, Kelly and I both noticed that her skin was black, and Kelly suspected that it might be second degree burns. The burns, though, were in fact hard packed dirt. Mary Sue's legs, feet, and hands were covered in so much dirt, that she looked like she had burns. For the second time that night, my heart broke. After a thorough and tough scrubbing, Mary Sue was asleep in her crib in our bedroom. Sarah, on the other hand, was not so easy to put to sleep. Kelly spent an hour cradling little Sarah, scared little Sarah, in her arms, rocking her to sleep. It wasn't easy, as Sarah screamed and cried herself to sleep. Sarah, though, wasn't the only one crying. Kelly was, too.

What kind of parents were these people? Who would allow their child to become so filthy? And who would leave their children in a hotel room by themselves? As I lay my head down on the pillow that night, my mind was a flood with questions, with no answers coming.

"Let's pray," Kelly said, as her hand reached across for mine, in the dark.

"Lord, thank you for placing Sarah and Mary Sue in our homes. Please give us the wisdom to look after these two, and to provide them what they need. Please allow them to sleep through the night, and please bless Linda, as well. Amen."

I decided to take the next day off work, and go shopping with Kelly and all five of the children for some clothes for our two newest family members. Getting everyone in the car, all seven of us, was a bit of a challenge, considering there were now three car seats, but we somehow managed. With the limited amount of money allotted to us by the state to buy the two girls clothes, it went fairly quickly. As it was growing late in the afternoon, and Kelly had to go to work later on that evening to massage some of her clients, we decided to go through a drive in and grab some food. While we were there, we were introduced to our next surprise with Sarah. A police car went sailing past us, siren splitting the mid day air with its screaming alert. It was at this point that Sarah began screaming, again, as well.

"Hide, hide, hide!" her high pitched wail screamed in intensity. "They're comin' ta get us! Hide!"

"Sarah, what's wrong? Who's coming?" My Australian wife was noticeably concerned, her mothering instincts taking over quickly.

"The bad guys are comin' ta get me. Hide!" she continued, her earsplitting scream shattering any semblance of calm.

"Sarah, honey, that noise is the police. They are good people, and they are going to help someone," I tried earnestly to reassure her.

"No they're not. That noise is the bad guys comin'. I have ta hide!" Her eyes pleaded with me, as her body seemed wracked with fear, struggling to get out of her car seat.

I tried to focus my attention on the drive home, while Kelly attempted to soothe Sarah's anxiety. The young four year old soon unraveled a tale I could not have envisioned. Our first foster child told us that when the police had come to her "house," or hotel room, her mother would hide her under the bed, and give her a knife, a "big knife," she said in order to protect herself. Whilst she told us this, her body continued to quake with fear, voice trembling, and her eyes remained wild.

"Kelly," I whispered across the car to her, "she is four years old. She can't be making these things up. What has she seen that could terrify her so?"

"I don't know, hon," Kelly silently said back to me. "And the knife part...what kind of home did she come from?" I wondered the same thing, myself.

I quickly came to dread visitations. Sarah and Mary Sue had their first visitation the following Tuesday with their "birth parents," a term foster parents used when referring to the natural parents. A visitation is when the foster child has a meeting with the birth parent, or parents, in a supervised location for up to two hours. Many times, this supervised location is at the local DFCS office or at a church. In the case of Sarah and Mary Sue, it was here in Monticello, at DFCS. It was up to Kelly or I to drop the two girls off and pick them up two hours later. It was the picking up the girls, and the aftermath that we didn't enjoy. In fact, these nights soon came to really disrupt our home life the most.

After arriving back in Monticello from my drive home from work in Eatonton, I drove to the DFCS office to pick up the two girls from their two hour visitation. As they were still with their parents, I waited in the lobby, glancing through a magazine. I didn't have to wait long, as I heard them coming long before I saw them. Both girls were in tears, with Sarah kicking and screaming down the hall, as Linda had to drag her to me.

"What's wrong?" I asked, as I quickly met Linda, taking Mary Sue in my arms, and bending down to Sarah, in an attempt to quiet her down.

"They just saw their mother, and didn't want to leave her," Linda said.

"How did their mom get here, if they don't have a car?" I was curious.

"A paid driver went and picked her up from the hotel. Dad's at work," was Linda's reply. "So many DFCS are low on state funds, due to cutbacks, and there is a shortage of caseworkers. As a result, many times, we, at DFCS, have to pay and train individual people to drive foster children and their birth parents to and from visitations, if there is a problem with transportation on either end. They're going to have visitations every Tuesday, at the same time."

"Okay, anything else I need to know?" I wondered.

"They've been fed. Mom gave Sarah cookies, chips, a hamburger, and a coke. Mary Sue just had a bottle. Also, there is a bag full of clothes and some toys for the kids upstairs, too."

I thanked Linda as she helped me put the crying girls in the car, and then grabbed the plastic bag of clothes and headed home. The ten minute drive home quickly put Mary Lou to sleep, as many babies seem to find car rides and humming engines soothing. Sarah was still hollering for her mother when we pulled into the driveway. As I got out of the car, I was met by my middle one, Jace, who was looking for her new sisters.

"What's wrong with Sarah, Daddy? Why is she crying?"

"Well, Jace, she just saw her mommy and she misses her," I tried to explain.

Now, my own children had been very helpful with the children, but I wasn't prepared for what Jace was about to do next. Without missing a beat, or with any guidance by me, Jace instantly took Sarah by the hand, led her into the house, saying to her, "Come on, Sarah, and let's go play with my dolls." In an instant, Sarah stopped crying; taking hold of Jace's outstretched hand, and followed her inside. I followed behind the two, holding Mary Sue in one arm, and my briefcase and plastic bag full from the birth mother in the other.

Kelly has a gift that I have not met in others. She can literally smell a problem a mile away. If there is a dead mouse anywhere in the house, she will be able to tell you the minute it died. So, when I walked up the stairs into the kitchen from the basement door, she wanted to know what was in the plastic bag. "Someone's been smoking," she said to me.

"How can you tell?"

"I can smell it," she assured me. "It's coming from that bag."

"There are clothes and toys from their mother and father in here. Linda gave it to me when I picked the kids up." We opened up the bag, and were greeted with a profoundly strong smell of smoke. Each article of clothing in the bag reeked of cigarette smoke. Along with this, the plush stuffed animals also were marinating in the same smell. Kelly swiftly took the bag out of my hand, dumped all of the contents into the wash machine, filled it with enough detergent to drive away any foul smell that ever existed anywhere on the clothes and dolls, and turned to me with a smile.

"They can't wear those clothes like that," she said.

When it came time for all of the children to go to bed, it was as if any progress we had made with Sarah had been erased. She kicked and screamed, shrieking for her mother, telling us that her mother told her and her sister that we weren't her parents and that we didn't love her. This, coupled with her dinner of cookies and coke, made it a very long evening indeed. By this time, Kelly and I had reverted back to our every other night schedule when our own three were babies, I have baby feeding and diaper changing one night, and she the next. This gave each of us a chance to get a full night's sleep every other night. Tonight was my night to attend to the children, and not only did Sarah scream for her mother, Mary Sue's body was not doing so well with whatever her mother fed her, as well. At least that's what her very full and dirty diaper and her screaming suggested to me. It was going to be a very long night.

"Well, I finally found Kolby's Easter candy," I told Kelly. It had been a month since Sarah and Mary Sue had come to live with us, with

Easter Sunday being two weeks ago. For our church's annual Easter Egg Hunt, held on Easter Saturday, we had bought all new Easter dresses for all four of our girls, as well as an Easter suit for Brody. Kelly and I were always very careful that our own children did not get too much candy of any kind, and that particular Saturday, we were on high alert that Sarah didn't get much at all. Every Tuesday evening, after the girls had visitation with their mother, they would always come back filled with both junk food and stories from their mother about how we didn't love them, how Sarah doesn't have to follow our rules and do what we say, and many other harmful suggestions.

Kolby's candy had been missing for roughly a week, now. As I was tucking Sarah into bed one night, I happened to lift up her pillow, and found a horde of Easter candy under it. Now, Sarah had already shown us a problem with candy. One afternoon, I found her in the pantry closet, slurping down a bottle of chocolate ice cream syrup. Another time, I found a potato chip bag under her bed. We had been told in foster parent training that foster children often have a problem with hoarding food. Sarah was absolutely fixated on food. Any time either Kelly or I would pop some food into our mouths, Sarah would instantly appear right next to us, many times popping out of thin air, it would seem, and stare at us, waiting to eat. Our training told us that many foster children came from homes where there was very little food, and this condition caused foster children to become fixated on food of any kind, often eating until they were sick. No matter how hard we tried to convince Sarah that she would always have enough food in our house, she would hide and store food away in her room whenever she had the chance. In the meantime, Mary Sue was putting on a lot of pounds, her ribs no longer showing like they did when she first came to live with us. She was an eating machine.

"Boom," Kelly's nickname for me, one that I received years ago, "I had a scary moment today when I picked up the girls from visitation." Kelly's voice was quivering, and I could see that she was visibly on the brink of tears. She soon spilled out a story that angered and scared me at the same time.

On this particular day, Kelly took the girls to a neighboring county and dropped them off at that county's DFCS, as the birth parents were unable to come to our town. While they had their visitation, Kelly and our three kids did some shopping while they waited, she told me, as she wiped away a tear from her eye. When it was time to pick up the girls, the two parents met her at the door of DFCS, as another caseworker placed Mary Sue in her arms, with Sarah crying beside her. Kelly then took the two girls out to the car, and tried to strap them in. What Kelly told me next really disturbed me.

"Boom, they followed me out to our car and started screaming at me," she said, her voice shaking. I quickly asked her what they were yelling, and she replied, "They were so angry, they were yelling that we are bad parents, that we don't deserve to have their children, and that they are the real parents. They stood right next to the car as I buckled Mary Sue in, and were just screaming at me. I was scared."

"What did you do?" I was upset! How dare them! Is this what it was going to be like to be foster parents? After all, we weren't the bad guys, I felt.

"I got in my car, and called Linda, and told her that the parents followed me to my car and started yelling at me. She just said not to worry unless they started to follow me," my wife answered. "I started to drive out of the parking lot, and they got in their car and followed."

"What?" I yelled. I was stunned, and I was worried. My wife and children should not have to be put through this. This was dangerous. After all, I thought, there is a reason why these people told Sarah that the police were the bad guys. Kelly was in danger!

"They followed me for a few blocks, but I was able to lose them in the traffic. Boom, it was awful!" Kelly exclaimed. I quickly went to hug her, trying to reassure and comfort her.

"Have you told Linda about this?"

"I did. She said that they will be talked to, and that they might not be able to have visitations again for a while."

I was mad; furious! I certainly didn't "sign up for this." If this was how visitations are going to be, I thought, Sarah and Mary Sue won't be able to attend them, as it was putting my family in danger. Something had to change.

It had been four months since the girls had come to live with us when we received another one of "the calls." This time, the call was not an arrival. Instead, it was about a departure. Mary Sue and Sarah were going to be leaving us, as their grandparents had received custody of them. I wasn't so sure how I felt about it. I was relieved on one hand, as it had been a strain on all of us taking care of them. Sarah had been acting mean towards Brody on more than one occasion, as she had been a very strong willed and independent little girl. She certainly knew what she wanted, and she was always quite determined to get it. There had been many discussions with her about taking food upstairs when we weren't looking. And those noisy scream filled nights after she had visitations! The whole house shook those nights. Sarah was very attached to her mother and truly missed her. Mary Sue, on the other hand, was simply too young to really understand her situation, and had not formed a strong attachment to her parents.

But, my concern lay with the children. I had a million questions for Linda about the grandparents. All of the questions regarded the future wellbeing and safety of the two. As a teacher, I had seen far too many children in rough situations and chilling home lives. How would it be for these two? What did the future bring for these two little girls who had come into our lives, our home, and our hearts?

Kolby, Jace, and Brody were upset. "Why do they have to leave us?" sprang forth from their lips the moment we sat down as a family to discuss it. I tried to tell them that God had plans for them, but tears were flowing freely between all three children. Kelly was upset the most. That night, she held Mary Sue in her arms, as she sat in the chair and cried. She had become very attached to both, particularly the baby. My wife, like most mothers I assume, had a soft spot for babies in her heart. What loving and decent mother doesn't, I thought. Yet, I was still upset with the birth mother, and was concerned that the parents might get the two back.

That night, while Kelly held Mary Sue, tears falling from her eyes, I was praying. I wasn't just praying for the girls and their grandparents, I was praying for myself, as well.

"God, thank you that these two girls were able to come into our lives. Lord, I ask that You keep them safe, and that You provide their grandparents with the wisdom, love, and the comfort that Sarah and Mary Sue need. Please keep these two girls from danger, and please hold them in Your loving arms throughout their lives. Heavenly Father, I also ask that You remove the bitterness and the frustration I hold towards the parents, and instead replace it with love, with Your love, as You love me. Amen."

Two months later, Kelly was nursing an aching heart towards the two. She was missing them tremendously. "Just call them," I urged her, as I went off to work. When I returned home that evening, she told me that the grandparents let her know that Mary Sue and Sarah were doing fine, and that Mary Sue was starting to crawl.

"I miss them, Daddy." Kolby looked up at me, with the innocent eyes of a seven year old. "Will we ever see them again?"

"I don't know, sweetheart. I hope so," I tried to assure her. I wanted to think that we would. I missed them, too.

CHAPTER 2

Being a "Yankee" and a "Foreigner" in our small town, Kelly and I are often asked about how we met, and why we ended up in Monticello, Georgia. I usually tell people that Kelly was looking up pictures of Tom Cruise or George Clooney on the internet and came across my picture. Truth is rather different, though. Short story….God. Long story, a little more detailed.

In June of 1989, I had finished my sophomore year at a small college in Michigan. I had been taking history and English classes, thinking about becoming a teacher, but really having no direction in my life. I was on a full music scholarship, singing in three choirs, and working as a DJ at the college radio station. Something had been greatly missing, but I wasn't sure what it was. I was in a funk. That's when the door of possibility opened up for me.

My mother took me to an Up With People concert, and what I saw during that two hour performance was rather impressive, though certainly not my style. I had been trained as a classical musician, performing in a renowned boy choir since the fourth grade. This was much different, as the group of 100 or so 18 to 28 year old performers from all corners of the globe put on a fantastic and upbeat song and dance show. So, I auditioned, and was accepted, travelling the world round in 1990. During the year, I met Kelly Heron from Australia, and immediately fell for her Aussie accent, her dynamic charm and personality, and her radiant smile. A month into the yearlong tour, I told her I had a crush on her. Funny thing, though; she ignored me for the next ten days, and I moved on….to a French girl for a bit, followed by an 8 month obsession with a Swede. Guess I couldn't find any American, or as the Europeans called them, Yankees, to fall for me. Together, Kelly, I, and 165 other people from 25 other countries performed on Good Morning America, in front of movie stars and Kings and Queens of Europeans countries, at the nearly fallen Berlin Wall, and crisscrossed the globe, performing for tens of thousands. It was an incredible experience and an astonishing year, and Kelly and I became dear friends, though romance was not in the picture at all. After all, I was chasing my Swede, and Kelly was involved with a lad from what was then West Germany.

The year came to a close, and we all went our separate ways. I spent a part of the next summer chasing the Swedish lass, yet to no avail. Kelly and I kept in touch, and she came to visit in November of 1991. Sparks flew, hearts were opened, and love was realized. We then spent the next two years bouncing between each other's respective countries for short visits, with long phone calls and even longer letters keeping us connected, before the internet and email, while I finished college with a teaching degree in history and English. After a brief period where Kel's old German flame came to Australia and tried to reclaim my Aussie's hand, Kelly and I were married in 1994 in her home town. I went to work as a substitute teacher, and as a manager of a skating rink and bowling alley, while Kelly earned her degree in linguistics and psychology.

The next two years flew by, and Kelly was thrilled about her first pregnancy. We were both excited for our first child. Kelly's faith in God was strong during this time, while I was just going through the motions. Kelly had always been resilient and solid in her devotion to God, while I was the opposite. I believed in God and tried to do the right thing, but I had not turned my life over to Him. I did pray over Kelly's tummy each night for a healthy, strong baby, though. Yet, God had other plans. Our first child, our daughter Bronte, died of Anencephaly, a condition where the brain fails to grow.

We were both devastated. Kelly surrounded herself with her family; I surrounded myself in my work. She sought God, I rejected him. She was sad, I was angry. Neither one of us had ever smoked, drank alcohol or taken drugs. Yet, we knew many people, some relatives on both sides, who did take drugs, who smoked, and who consumed alcohol, and they had healthy, living babies. The irony was too much for me. God was not real. I was done with Him, believing that He had rejected me.

So, we escaped life. Kelly had just earned her degree, and I was in a job that was unfulfilling. We sold our things, packed up a few clothes, and moved to Great Kepple Island, a tropical island in the middle of the Great Barrier Reef for just under a year, working for the owners of the island, Quantas, an Australian airline business. All of our meals were cooked three times a day by chefs, there were no bills, and we lived on the Great Barrier Reef. It was beautiful, and it was the exact place we needed to be in order to mend our shattered hearts. After what constituted about a year there, we moved back to "the mainland," as our second child, Kolby was born. I was still angry with God, and would not allow Kolby to be baptized in a church. Instead, Kolby was baptized in Kelly's mother's backyard. It was at this point that Kelly encouraged me to follow my dream. Well, actually, she told me we had to do it, as she didn't want a husband having a mid life crisis later on in life. So, we moved back to America with a three week old baby, with no car, with no job, and with no house. What we did have were only my dream, and Kelly's faith.

The dream was....professional wrestling. Ever since a child, I had been enamored with the sport. And, since I weighed only 135 pounds, I wasn't going to be a wrestler any time soon. That led me to dreaming of becoming a manager, or the individual who managed the bad guys, insulted the crowd on the microphone to get the crowd to boo him, and help him to cheat when the referee wasn't looking. It was all I thought about doing, all I read about, and it consumed me. Therefore, Kelly told me to get it out of my system, though she hated it. She probably hated it as much as I loved it. But, she believed in me, and with that in mind, we flew into Atlanta, Georgia in June of 1997, and eventually ended up in Monticello, a tiny rural town. Kelly and I have jokingly called Monticello "Mayberry" since the day we walked into the town's barbershop. As we had only been in town for three months and had just found a church, we didn't know really anyone in town by name, yet. We lived "out in the sticks," so to speak, outside of the two stop light, small rural town, and, as the locals say, "out yonder in the woods." Kelly, Kolby, and I walked into the barbershop on a Saturday morning, and it was like walking into Floyd's barbershop on the Andy Griffith Show, complete with six people in the shop, and only one there to get a haircut, as the others were there to catch up on the latest news and gossip. When Kelly introduced herself, one local said "I know who you are; you're the ones from Australia." I quickly looked for Barney Fife at that point. The town is so gloriously and wonderfully small that everyone knows everyone else, a great place to settle down and raise a family. Whether it is walking into one of the town's two banks, the grocery store, or the local hardware store, both Kelly and I are always greeted by name and with a smile.

I did the wrestling thing for three years, until the birth of Jace. During this time, my faith was restored, and I eventually gave my life over to Christ, seeking ways to serve Him at every opportunity, and Kelly and I became heavily involved in our church. I was teaching English and Drama at the high school level, while Kelly went back to school to gain another degree, this time as a massage specialist. Our son, Brody also joined our family, and life was firing on all cylinders. We were busy, and we were happy.

For some time at work, I had been puzzled as to why some of the students had been acting the way they had. I had come across far too many that were not at all concerned about their grades, and who were disrespectful towards both their fellow students and to teachers. I often wondered where these problems came from until I either spoke to the parents, or, on rare occasion, met them. Sadly, there were too many children coming from homes where parents, or on many occasions, a single parent, just wasn't interested in the child's grades or progress. Or, there were those children whose parents were too busy to be involved in their child's school work. And then there were those parents I met who were just simply....mean spirited. They were rude to their children, rude to others, and rude to me. I don't mind them being rude to me, as I can handle it. But when a parent is out-and-out mean to the child, it hurts all involved.

Yet, what I found most disturbing, though, happened when I was a 32 years old. I met the mother of one of my seniors who was failing English class. Her daughter was 17 years of age, and pregnant. That was disturbing unto itself. What really shook me that day was that the student's mother was younger than I was. I just wasn't ready for that. Sure, I knew that it would come, one day, but I was only 32, and this mother of a student, a 17 year old student, was younger than I was. And, she was about to be a grandmother! "It's not supposed to be like this!" my mind screamed. "This is just not right! How is this student of mine going to make it through life? What about college? How can she take care of a baby when she is a child herself?" The fact that someone could be a grandparent at my age also alarmed me. "Grandparents are OLD! Or, at least they are SUPPOSED to be." My mind was a momentary train wreck. All of my preconceptions of normality were derailed, and I had some heavy duty thinking to do. So, as I stumbled home that night after work, the first thing I asked Kelly was, "Sweetheart, what would you think if we adopted a baby?"

"Just make sure you have enough diapers," she responded. Her answer was not what I expected. We both had come to the same conclusion after Brody was born, we were done, no more babies in the house. However, I had been thinking a lot about the foster program. I mentioned this to Kelly, but she was not interested. "Maybe," she said. "We'll have to find out more about it and pray about it."

A month later, at our town's annual Deer Festival in November, we came across a Foster Parent booth, with information about the program. "Maybe," Kelly said again, "we'll have to pray about it." I signed our names up to be contacted for training information, anyway. I have always been the type of person who once I have my mind on something, I run with it. I have very little patience for waiting. So, I started calling our local Department of Family and Children's Services, known as DFCS, about training hours. It turned out that training was set to begin in January of the following year, 2003. "I don't know, Boom," Kelly said about the training, "I don't know if I am ready for that. It's a big commitment, you know; huge. I'll go to one training meeting, but I'm not committing." She was adamant. At least I was getting her in the door.

"Kelly, if we can help just of one of these kids, it's worth it. We are blessed with so much from God, I want to share these blessings," I pleaded. I strongly felt that way. The past four summers, I had spent part of my vacation building homes for people in Mexico as part of a church mission trip. The missions had changed my life, as I saw close up the living conditions of children in third world countries, children who lived in squalor, had nothing to call their own, yet had such infectious smiles and jubilant laughter. In fact, after I returned home the first summer after my initial mission house building trip, I was so overcome with guilt that I was in a funk for a few weeks. How could I, who felt so unworthy, have so much, when others lived without electricity, running water, solid walls, and nevertheless live with so much joy and not complain? Perhaps being a foster parent would allow me to share my full blessings with other children. After all, I believed, these children didn't need to suffer because of the bad choices of their parents.

We mentioned to a few friends what we were planning to do, as well as some family members, and did not receive the response I expected. Some asked us why we would do it. Others questioned our sanity. Still others looked at us as if we had penguins flying out of our noses. Perhaps I had taken a few too many chair shots to the head during my days in professional wrestling. What was perhaps most disappointing was the response I received from some of my own family, and continue to receive. "John, why are you doing this? You're too busy," were words I heard, and continue to hear, from them. Too busy? Sure, Kelly and I were busy then, when we considered training. We had three young children, I had a full time job, and Kelly had a full time job, as well, plus the added responsibility of running her own business. Yet, there was clearly a need for foster parents. When we visited the booth during the Deer Festival, the foster parents attending to the booth told Kelly and me that our small county was short on foster parents. We could do it, I reassured Kelly. Let's just give the training a try, and then go from there. I arranged for Lindsey, our cherished baby sister, to look after our three kids, as the training sessions were every other Tuesday evening, lasting for three hours. Lindsey had started babysitting for us when she was ten years of age. Kolby was a nine months old at the time, and Kelly had begun working at the church part time as a secretary. From time to time, Kelly would ask Lindsey to watch over Kolby in the church nursery while Kelly worked across the hallway in the office. Since then, Lindsey had become part of the family, and the best baby sitter I knew. When we would come home from a night out, Lindsey would have all three kids in bed asleep, the kitchen cleaned from one end to the other, and the dirty clothes washed, dried, and folded on top of our bed.

So, with Lindsey at the house, we went to our first foster parent training session. Neither one of us knew what to expect. "I wonder if we will know anybody there," I said aloud.

"Probably not," was all Kelly said. She, too, wondered what we would find.

We walked into the county's DFCS building at 6:00 that cold, windy Tuesday night, and were told to go upstairs to the conference room. We took the elevator up and walked into the room, where we were met by three other couples. Kelly was right, we didn't know anybody there. After some pleasant introductions, we met Sandra, a DFCS case manager, and our trainer throughout the six month process. Sandra then had us all tell a little bit about each other, with each couple explaining why they wanted to foster. Each couple there had a different story to tell, though each story centered on the theme of wanting to help children. One couple, Jason and Tammy, already had a son in high school, and were looking to help other children, as they felt called by God to do so. Another couple, Lori and Joe, wished to go through the foster to adopt process, in which a foster child is eventually adopted by the foster family. William and Laura had some friends who were foster parents, and were curious about becoming foster parents, themselves. The one thing we all had in common was that we wanted to help children.

The evening went rather smoothly, and I quickly had many of the others laughing with my jokes. For some reason, anytime I am in a serious meeting of any kind, my mind starts to race away from me as jokes form in my brain. The main problem lies in that I don't have a very good filter, and jokes start to fall out of my mouth. Kelly is rather used to it, as are my own children, bur for these strangers, as well as Sandra, well, they weren't sure if I was serious or not. I tend to joke around with a serious face.

"Why do you want to become a foster parent? What drew you to the program?" were Sandra's initial questions to us.

"Well, I was looking for some more children to work around the house for us, and I thought that with these foster children, I would be able to work around the child and slave labor laws. I am curious, though," I said, with my face not cracking a smile, "will my six months in jail be a hindrance, at all? I mean, I was only caught by the police just the one time."

Sandra let out a nervous laugh. Some of the others looked down. "Don't mind him," Kelly said, "he's joking. He does it all the time. He can't help it." With this, Jason let out a strong laugh, and I knew that I had made a friend right away. For the rest of the evening, I let the jokes fly. That is, until I got the look from Kelly. It was the look that told me that enough was enough. I had accomplished my mission, though, as I had brought an air of friendliness and relaxation to the room and to our meeting. Shoulders eased from release of stress, and all started to open up more, putting fears and nerves to rest.

Sandra put us through some role playing exercises, followed by a video interview of some foster parents. As it was close to 9:30 that night, it was time to head for home. Sandra gave us a stack of papers. I believe I strained my back picking up them off the desk. It seemed as if I had the entire works of Shakespeare handed to me. "These are forms that you need to have filled out by next time. There are police back ground checks, release forms, and other information forms in there."

We said our goodbyes to everyone and headed to the car. "Well, what do you think?" I was anxious to know what Kelly thought of the meeting. After all, if she didn't want to be a foster parent, there was no use continuing going to the meetings. We had both decided long ago in our marriage that we were going to be partners in all we did, 50-50. So, if one of us wasn't on board with being a foster parent, than both of us weren't going to be on board. I studied her carefully.

"It was okay. I really like the others. Tammy and Lori seem so nice."

"Yeah, they sure are. And Jason seemed to enjoy my jokes. You want to go back in two weeks?" I asked.

"Yes, but I'm still not sure I want to do this," she replied.

The next two weeks went by quickly. We filled out all the paper work, got our finger prints taken care of, and went about the usual day to day routine, at least whatever routine one can have with three young children. Brody was only two years old at the time, and Kelly was just getting her massage business up and going, working in the evenings when I would return home from work. We were both adamant about not placing our own children in day care, as we felt that it was more important to sacrifice financially and not have two full time jobs in order for her to stay home during the day and raise our children.

Before we knew it, two weeks had passed, and we were at the next foster training session. Sandra opened up the session by asking us if we had any questions from the previous meeting, and I looked at her, deadpan and straight faced, and asked "Will these meetings be catered by chefs from outside our county, or from here in Monticello." Jason immediately laughed. I knew I liked him.

Kelly just groaned, and gave her usual reply when I was making a joke, "Just ignore him, please."

Sandra spent the evening discussing with us the reasons why children were placed into foster care. We heard stories about children who were neglected, who were abused, and who were abandoned. "Many times," Sandra told us, "these children are placed with us because of parental abuse." She then wove a tale of various forms of physical, emotional, and mental abuse that disturbed me deeply. I had read about child abuse for years, but never really spent much time in thought about it, as I had never really come face to face with it, or at least recognized it for what it was. That was it, I soon discovered. I had always been around children who had been abused, as many of them sat in my classroom each day, I just never realized it.

"And, what happens to these children once they are in foster care?" I put the question out to Sandra, though it was on the minds of all of us. "Do they ever go back to the family?" I was hoping the answer was no.

"Reunification is what we always work towards," she responded. Seeing by our faces that many of us weren't familiar with that term, Sandra went on to explain further. "Reunification is when the birth parents fulfill all of their responsibilities to DFCS and to the court and are able to have their children returned to them. The parents have twelve months in which they have to take parenting classes, find a stable job, and a home. Also, during this time, they can have no arrests. Many times they may have to take counseling sessions, as well. If, after the twelve months have passed, and they have not fulfilled these responsibilities, they have their parental rights taken away from them."

"Then, do the foster parents adopt the children?" Tammy wanted to know.

"No, DFCS then searches for family members who are interested in adopting the child. After an exhaustive search is made, and it is found that there is no family member willing to adopt the child, the foster parents have the first right to adopt. If the foster parents don't wish to adopt the child, the child is placed on an adoption list. Sometimes, though, they move into a group home for older children." I remembered that Joe and Lori wanted to adopt a child. From the sounds of what Sandra had to say, it could be a long wait for the two of them.

The next session saw us performing in a role playing scenario. Joe, Jason, and I played the part of foster child, birth parent, and caseworker. I was the birth parent, and I embraced the opportunity to perform in front of my small audience, pretending to be the bad guy, the villain, and really hamming it up. Jason and Joe both laughed, and tried to follow my lead, Jason as the child, and Joe as the caseworker. Though I played the part of the birth parent over the top and with exaggeration, I believed in my heart that the birth parents were often the bullies and the "bad guys," while their own, precious children were repeatedly the "victims." Surely after all Sandra told us, there was some truth to this. I had expressed these feeling to Kelly before, and she had, very correctly, reminded me that God does not want us to judge others. After all, James 4:12 clearly asked me "But you, who are you to judge your neighbor?" Yet, it was hard. How could parents treat their own children in such horrific manners? It was just beyond my understanding.

The months passed, and training came to an end. We had numerous discussions on diversity in families, forms of abuse, and stages of grief due to being separated from one's family. We were now ready to foster. The next step was the one beyond our control, though. That was the one where we simply had to wait for the phone call; the call asking us if would take a child into our home. Kelly and I had informed DFCS that we didn't want to foster any children that were older than Kolby, as we didn't want to introduce our children to some beliefs, actions, and language from older foster children; children who had been through many different experiences than or our own children, at that young stage in their lives.

Spring had come once more to Monticello, and the daffodils were in bloom all around our house. I had begun the tradition of planting 200 daffodil bulbs every winter throughout our yard, and we were now surrounded by white, yellow, and orange flowers showing off their colorful bonnets. The air was filled with the songs of birds, as they attended to their construction of their homes. Over the years, since our return back to America, my love of gardening and bird feeding had become much stronger. In fact, one of the reasons Kelly and I had built our new home, our second in Monticello, was purely due to the fact that we had run out of garden space out at our old home. While Kelly designed our new home, I designed the garden beds on our six acres, and spring time was my favorite time of year to be outside and get my hands in the soil.

"Kelly, what do you think about getting chickens?" I asked her. "We could have fresh eggs every day." I knew this would grab her. Kelly was becoming a titanic advocate for healthy food, and we had begun to seriously look more and more to organic foods.

"That would be neat. The kids could collect eggs every morning for breakfast. We could have lots of omelets." I was ecstatic! I had sold her on the idea of chickens not really for the eggs, but for the manure for my gardens, though I didn't let on, whatsoever, that this was the idea.

"Great!" I'll start building a coop this weekend," I said. By that weekend, I had cleared out a space, bought the materials, and began construction of my first coop. It was going to be the envy of all chicken farmers. It was the cathedral of chicken coops. Chickens would be squawking to get into this plush place. I leapt into action that Saturday morning.

As I hammered and painted, I thought and prayed. "God, are we up to fostering? It's going to be hard. We look to You for all things, and we lean upon You for strength. Please use us to help others. But, Lord, I don't want someone who is going to be hard on our family. Please bring the right match to our house, someone who will fit in with all of us, someone who our children can love and help as well. Amen." I spent the rest of that day building the chicken coop, completely unaware that the hardest years of my life were straight ahead of me.

CHAPTER 3

Cross continental marriages are a little tougher in some aspects. That's how I describe our marriage to others; "cross continental." Kelly and I are from not only two different countries, we are from two different continents. I know a man at work who jokes that his wife ought to be from another world, as she is from Tennessee, and he is from Georgia. Then there are those couples who are quite serious when they say that they have a hard time visiting all of their in-laws during the holiday seasons when one set of in-laws live in one state and the other set lives in a nearby state. Now, I know I should have some sympathy for these road weary couples who have to cross over state lines during the Christmas vacation period. But, I can't seem to muster up any.

Kelly and I constantly face the challenge of always having one of us living in not only a different state, but in a foreign country. Either she or I will always live half a world away from the nearest blood relative. I admit that Kelly has taken up this cross much better than I, as we have lived in my country the past several years. Kelly was raised by her mother, and it was just the two of them, as Kelly was the only child. At the same time, she was also raised alongside a gaggle of cousins. Or, would that be a pride of cousins? Whatever the group name might be, she was part of a very large, very loving extended family that she grew very fond of, very close with, something I did not have in my life as I was growing up. Living half a world away from those she grew up with has been very hard on her. Even more so, it has been hard on her mother, as my mother in law's only grandchildren are a very long, very expensive plane trip away. After all, it is pretty much impossible to go to Australia for the weekend to visit grandma. It takes a weekend just to get there by plane.

This distance has caused some strain in our marriage. The expense, the distance, and the time spent away from one's family is extremely hard. Along with that is the guilt placed upon the shoulders of the one living far away from home. When I moved to Australia, my mother was a wreck, thinking she would never see me again. Kelly's mother was the same way when we moved here. This added burden can be emotionally draining on the one living away, and a challenge both must face together, or the marriage suffers. Looking back, God knew exactly what He was doing when He brought us to Monticello. We have been able to carve out our own identity, far from both my family and hers. If we had lived in Michigan, close to my parents, I believe that Kelly would have not been able to shine on her own as much as she has. My wife is amazing, though. Most of our friends have no clue that she is always homesick, as Kelly makes all seem at ease when she is around. She places herself last in all she does, and has the gift to make everyone she speaks to feel special. I imagine this is a large reason for her success as a massage therapist. People simply enjoy being around Kelly.

Since the plane tickets are very expensive to fly to Australia, added to the great length of time it takes to get there and back, we tend to turn our vacations there into long ones. Kelly prefers to take the kids with her, so they can visit Grandma and the other aunts, uncles, and cousins that come from all over the Land Down Under to spoil them with love, hugs, and kisses. Sometimes I am able to go, if work allows. Other times, Kelly only goes by herself, if the kids are in school. If she is lucky, Kelly makes it back home every year and a half to two years, with her mother coming in between those times for a visit. Yet, it is an adventure being married to someone from another country. Kelly and I both share a love of travel and discovery. Along with this, we both experienced so much world traveling during our year in Up With People, and crave to do more of it. Our children, too, have a better understanding of the world than most their age, and all have traveled extensively in their short lives. Plane trips are as familiar as automobiles, while airports seem like a second home to them. Travel is in our blood. Fostering, it seems, would also creep into our blood, as well.

Sarah and Mary Sue had left our house in May of 2004. The summer came and went. I spent much of it in the garden and taking care of the kids, while Kelly spent a great deal of time at work. Clearly one of the benefits of being a teacher was having summer vacation with the children. This was the first summer I had not traveled to Mexico to build houses. The previous summer, I had spent five weeks there, managing the construction, as churches from across the United States came to do mission work. My job as a teacher allowed me significant time in the summer to follow God's calling in this. Now, I felt God was calling me to be a foster parent, a mission unto itself, as Kelly and I were about to find out with our next child.

Kelly was in Australia with Brody visiting family, while Kolby, Jace, and I stayed home. School had just begun in the first week of August, and Jace was beginning her first year, in Kindergarten, while Kolby was already a seasoned pro at school, beginning this year in the second grade. The first two weeks saw no major incident that I couldn't attend to in my role as Daddy in Charge. I enjoyed the roles of both Mr. Dad and Mr. Mom. When the girls went to bed each night, I did the dishes, laundry, cleaning, and made their lunches for the next day. No worries, as my Aussie bride would often say. I missed her, but I was glad that she was able to spend time with her mother and family.

One night after school, the phone rang. "Hello, Mr. DeGarmo, this is Barbara from DFCS. How are you doing?"

"I'm good, thanks for asking. How are you?" My heart jumped a beat. Was this THE call?

"Fine, thank you. We have a girl, from Jasper County, who is in need of a home. Are you able to take her in at this time?"

Whoa! I wasn't ready for this. There was NO way in the world that I was either capable or brave enough to make that decision all on my own, without Kelly's input. Maybe brave was not the right choice of words. Perhaps, foolish might be more fitting. Besides, this was something that we very much needed to pray about. I told Barbara this and also asked for some information about the girl, so I could discuss it with Kelly on the phone later that evening.

"Well, her name is Sydney. She is seven years old. She lives with her grandmother right now. Grandma is an alcoholic, and is unable to provide for Sydney. Sydney suffers from neglect. She doesn't have any severe learning difficulties that we are aware of, and is, for the most part, well behaved. The placement would probably be only for a weekend, as we are working on getting her a permanent place to live with an aunt and uncle. Talk to Kelly, and let me know, please, as soon as you can. Thanks."

I was outside on our porch, overlooking the creek that flows through our property. The creek was surrounded by trees on both sides, many of them fallen and decaying with age. The songs of birds filled the air, as squirrels capered about throughout the emerald foliage. I glanced at my watch; it was 4:37 in the afternoon my time. That meant it was 7:37 AM in Australia, the following morning for Kelly. I said a silent prayer, thanking God for the beauty of my surroundings, and for insight from Him in this, and then called Australia. This was Thursday, and Kelly would be home the following Monday, so she probably wouldn't even meet this newest foster child. Still, I needed her insight, and of course, her approval. Kelly's mother, Shirley, answered the phone, and it was evident that I had awoken her. "Hey, Shirl, it's Boom. I'm so sorry to wake you up, but I need to speak with Kelly about something, if you don't mind."

"Oh, hi Boom. Sure thing, I'll get her for you. She's still asleep, so it might take a sec."

"Hey hon," Kelly's sleepy voice was like the sweetest music to my ears. I missed her, and just hearing her voice always seemed to make the worst problem instantly better for me. Maybe I was addicted to it. "What's the matter? Mom said you needed to talk to me about something."

"Kel, I'm sorry to wake you, but I just got off the phone with a caseworker from DFCS, named Barbara. There's a seven year old from Monticello who is suffering from neglect, and she needs a place to stay. The caseworker told me it would probably just be for the weekend."

"Where will she go after that?" From the tone of Kelly's voice, she had become fully awake by this point.

"Apparently, there are some family members who are trying to get custody of her. It's no problem for me, I can handle it, and Kolby and Jace can help out. Besides, it's just for the weekend."

"I'm not sure, Boomie. Let's pray about it," she said, and I agreed. This time, Kelly took the lead. "Dear God. We are facing a big decision here, and we need Your help in this. Please let us know what You would have us do. Amen."

A wave of reassurance passed over me as Kelly finished voicing her prayer, and I felt good about taking Sydney into our home. Besides, I told myself, it's only for a couple of days. Surely I can handle that. No worries. "You already said "yes," didn't you," Kelly said.

"No, I didn't." I wanted to, was it that obvious to her? "What do you think about it?" I was ready to call Barbara back; I just needed Kel's okay on this.

"If you think its okay," she said, hesitatingly.

"Kel, I feel good about it. It won't be a problem. Don't worry about it, we can handle it. Sorry to wake you, hon. Try to go back to sleep, and I will see you Monday night. I'll be praying you all the way home. Love ya."

"Love you, too. See you Monday. Give the girls a kiss for me," she said.

I hung up the phone, and called Barbara back, praying for God's strength in this as I dialed the number. "Barbara, hi, this is John. I just got off the phone with Kelly. We are good to go. We can take her."

"Great," Barbara said. I could hear the sense of relief in her voice. "I'll bring her by tomorrow after school. I have to get her things while she's at school, and then I'll pick her up from school and bring her to your house. Like I said, it might just be for the weekend. Thanks, John, I appreciate it."

After I hung up, my mind started to run away with what I had to get done for the weekend. To begin with, we needed a place for her to stay for the few nights. Brody's room! Of course! It came to me quickly, we still had that extra bed in Brody's room, and he won't be here until

Monday, so no problem, there. We were going to need some extra food, though for the next few days. Did I hear Barbara right, I thought to myself? She just didn't say, "it MIGHT just be for the weekend"? "Might?" I must have heard it wrong. But, even if I didn't, she just said that because she had to officially cover all the bases, so to speak. I didn't give it a second thought. Instead, I called Kolby and Jace downstairs.

"Girls," I said, as they came into the kitchen, "we are going to get a foster child tomorrow and..."

I was interrupted immediately by the girls jumping up and down, howling at the same time. "Who is it?" Kolby squealed.

"Is it a girl?" Jace, who was usually very, VERY quiet, was a bundle of unbridled enthusiasm. The last time she looked this happy was when Santa Claus visited our house last Christmas.

"Yes, Jace, it's a girl, and her name is..."

"A sister, a sister!" I was having a hard time finishing sentences. The girls were now jumping again. Didn't we just go through this a few months back with Sarah and Mary Sue?

"Her name is Sydney, and she is seven years old. She is going to be very sad when she comes to live with us, so we need to help her out. Can you do this?" They both shook their heads enthusiastically. I was certain that Sydney would be very confused and frightened when she came to us, as she was to be picked up straight after school from the caseworker. "Great, thanks girls. Now, go get your shoes on, and let's go to the grocery store and get some food for Sydney." They scrambled up the stairs, giggling all the way up. My children are my heroes, I thought to myself, as they are wonderful with foster children.

I was glad to see Barbara when she arrived later the next day, for I had had a hard time focusing on my teaching throughout the morning. My mind was wandering with all sorts of questions about Sydney, and I was happy for the school day to end. Better yet, its one day closer to Kelly getting home, I thought to myself. "Daddy, Daddy! She's here!" Kolby came running into my bedroom with a thousand mile grin. Both she and Jace had been watching out the window for the car to arrive. I rushed to meet Barbara and Sydney outside.

"Hey, Barbara, I'm John. It's nice to meet you. Thanks for coming," I said, as I extended my hand out to greet her. I took the black plastic bag from Barbara, and bent down to say hello to Sydney. I was expecting a terrified, crying child.

"Hi! Are you my new daddy?" She looked up at me with the largest grin I had seen in some time. Her face was smeared in dirt, and her hair had not been washed in what looked like weeks, maybe months. I wondered if a comb had ever graced her long blonde hair. Her clothes were also filthy, and appeared to be about two sizes too small. Yet, her smile told me that this was not a scared child. She appeared....happy. Surely, I was wrong.

I wasn't really sure how to handle her question. I wanted to make her feel comfortable and reassure her, but at the same time, I didn't want to give her false hope. "Ah...." I stammered, trying to find the right words, "my name is Mr. John. Are you Sydney?"

"Yeah," she said, between some missing teeth. Instantly, her infectious attitude was winning me over. This was going to be a different experience than with Sarah and Mary Sue.

"Sydney, it's really nice to meet you. Thank you for coming to stay with us." I tried to make her feel at ease, but it looked like she already was. "This is Kolby, and this is Jace. Kolby is seven years old, just like you, and Jace is five." My two girls were standing a little away from us, and weren't sure what to make of Sydney just yet. I had prepared them for a crying and screaming child. Sydney was anything but that. "Girls, let's take Sydney inside and get her something to eat."

"Yeah, c'mon!" Sydney took Kolby and Jace both by the hands and led the way in, Barbara and I followed her lead. This is going to be easy, I thought.

Kolby and Jace helped me get something for Sydney to drink, and the three of them sat at the table in the kitchen. As I left the room and entered into our parlor to do the paperwork with Barbara, I watched as Kolby and Jace sat across from their temporary new foster sister, wide eyed with curiosity, while Sydney talked a mile a minute, with a smile stretched from ear to ear.

Barbara was older and leaning towards retirement and was cold and businesslike in her approach. She gave me just the facts about Sydney, and spared any emotional connection to her, different from what we experienced with Sandra, but nothing I couldn't handle. After all, this was just for a weekend. Barbara went on to tell me that Sydney had been feeding herself hotdogs from the microwave at home for pretty much every meal, as her grandmother was too hung over to provide any meals. When Sydney did get to school, it was because she dressed herself and got herself to the bus stop on time. Her attendance at school was poor, no doubt as a result of situation, I thought to myself. As I listened to Barbara, I heard Sydney laughing wildly. Good sign. "What about the family members? When will they be getting Sydney?" This was just going too simple, a trouble free weekend.

"Well, Mr. DeGarmo, there's a holdup on that. They won't be able to take Sydney after this weekend. I'm not sure how long she will be under care, but we'll let you know. Is this going to be a problem?" Very businesslike, Barbara leveled her gaze right at me.

"Sure, it shouldn't be a problem." After all, it was supposed to be just for the weekend. How much longer could it take? A couple of days? A week? I'm sure Kelly would say the same thing.

We finished the paperwork, and I thanked Barbara again for bringing Sydney over as we walked to the door. After she left, I walked to the kitchen to find my two girls a little more relaxed, though still puzzled over Sydney. Kolby and Jace were two reserved girls, and Jace just didn't talk much, in general. Jace was very much the observer in our family, always watching others, while Kolby was the social butterfly of our fivefold family. Both looked up at me, with confused grins on their angelic faces. Sydney was the life of the room, arms waving here and there, and ready to fall off her chair at any second, as peals of laughter bellowed forth from her small frame. From her boney arms and legs, it was obvious that she had not been well fed. "Girls, let's show Sydney her new room," I said, taking Sydney's belongings with one hand, and Sydney's outstretched hand in my other.

"Geez, you sure do have a nice house, daddy," she said, as we walked upstairs to Brody's room.

"......thank you," I replied. Kolby glanced over at me, confused. I wasn't so comfortable with this daddy thing, myself. Is this healthy, I wondered.

Sydney was filthy dirty when it was bath time. When was the last time she had a bath? Her hair was dense with grime and grease, almost impenetrable, and required a large dose of shampoo. She continued to laugh and squeal in the tub, pretty much emptying the tub with her splashing. It was at this time that I noticed that she was also skin and bones, with each rib visibly showing. Afterwards, we sat down for dinner. Friday has traditionally been pizza night at our house, and we enjoyed Kolby's favorite, pepperoni, followed by some homemade cookies and cream ice cream. Since our marriage, I had become quite a connoisseur of ice cream flavors, as well as an expert in making it. My favorite wedding gift in Australia had been an ice cream maker, and it was one of the first purchases I made when returning back to the states. Sure, it wasn't the healthiest meal for Sydney on her first night, but I was tired, it was late, and it was Friday. Pizza it is, I thought. Sydney devoured it, shoveling down bite after bite at a sprinter's pace. Either she enjoyed pizza, or this was her first meal in some time. Probably both, I considered.

We said our nightly prayers, asking for God to be with Brody and Kelly, and to prepare their hearts and body for the long trip home, and then I tucked the girls into the separate beds, with Sydney first. "Good night, Daddy," she said, through sleepy eyes. It had been an exhausting day for all of us.

"Good night, Sydney, sleep well. I'm glad you are here with us. Jesus loves you," I said, as I brushed back wisps of hair from her face.

"Who's that?" she asked.

I had taken it for granted that Sydney knew about Jesus. Guess not. "Jesus is God's son, and He loves you very much." I crept downstairs, cleaned the kitchen and washed the dishes. After this, I emptied Sydney's clothes out of the plastic bag. I was directly hit by the stench of cigarette smoke. Ugh! It was overpowering! Each article was permeated with the odor. These clothes needed two washings, I told myself, to get rid of this stench. Her poor lungs, I thought.

At the bottom of the bag was an oddly shaped pink pillow, not quite round, and stained with mud and dirt. It also reeked of the same smell. As I was about to toss it into the wash machine for a reviving cleanse, something caught my eye. Why, it was a picture pillow. This worn and grubby pillow had a plastic sleeve where a small picture could be inserted. Pretty neat; hadn't seen one of those before, I thought. Taking the picture out, there before me was image of an old, leathery faced woman, lined with crow's feet and furrows. The haunting dark eyes were filled with sadness, and the yellow toothless smile was one of great weariness. This was a picture of someone who had been through a great many hardships in life, I surmised, and who was aged beyond her years. The inscription on the back was etched in shaky handwriting, reading "To Sydney, I love you, Granny". It was a frightening glimpse into Sydney's life, as I came to better understand her plight. This young girl placed in my home was a victim of her environment. Yet, she seemed to be filled with such happiness and optimism, her laughter still humming in my ears. I set the picture on the counter, and placed the pillow into the washing machine, giving all the contents the strongest cleaning cycle the machine had to offer. Afterwards, I went downstairs and relaxed in front of the TV with a DVD of my favorite actor, Bela Lugosi. Dear Bela, he always helps me to unwind, as I lose myself in his flicks. I saw the credits open the film, and then was fast asleep.

The weekend had come and gone without much trouble at all. Saturday was spent making sure the house was ready for Kelly when she got home, and the girls helped out, Sydney pitching right in. I began to notice that she had a very loud voice, at times, ear piercing in her shrillness. She was excited and happy, and complied peacefully with all that was asked of her. Saturday was Pancake Day in our house, and she wolfed those down like no one's business. It was the same for lunch and dinner. If I wasn't careful, I would be sending her back to her family members twelve sizes larger. Sunday was spent in church, and Kolby graciously shared one of her church dresses with Sydney. As always, our church family enfolded her quickly with loving outreach. I did have to check in on her during Sunday School class, as I could hear her high pitched laughing down the hallway.

"Don't worry, John, she's fine," her Sunday School teacher told me.

When Monday morning rolled around, I took all three girls to school before heading off to work. Even though Sydney was a few months older than Kolby, she was in the first grade, as she had been retained from the previous year. "Sydney, honey, who is your teacher? What is her name?" I needed to know what room to take her to in the small, rural school.

"I da know."

"You don't know the name of your teacher?"

"No, sir."

"Okay.....well, do you know where your room is?" We were just pulling into the school, and needed to know quickly, as I was running a bit late this morning; not used to getting three girls ready for school in the early morning. Two girls I had down pat, and could do with no problems. Three? Well, that was a different story.

"Yeah." Her smile was a little brighter after having her teeth brushed in what was probably the first time in quite a stretch.

"Yes sir," I corrected her, as it was a force of habit from being an English teacher.

"Yes sir," she said, leading the way. I made my introduction to the teacher, and took Jace and Kolby to their classes, and then off to my own school, for a long day of work. Long, because I was anxious to see Brody and cover my wife's face with kisses. I had missed them, and always feel a little empty when my wife and best friend is not around.

"Do you think Mommy's plane is here yet?" Kolby asked. We were driving to the airport in Atlanta, a place which was quickly becoming a second home to us with visitors from Australia and Michigan coming and going on a regular basis.

"Not yet, Kolb. Brody and Mommy will be there soon. They are still in the air, flying on the plane. If you look up, maybe one of those planes flying above us will be them." My kids had flown so many times; planes were already passé to them. Not so to Sydney.

"Wow! Look at that, daddy!" she shrieked. "There's another one!" she shouted, unable to contain herself. Her excitement filled the car, as Kolby and Jace began to giggle. We were close to the airport, as the giant 747s and other colossal planes thundered over our car. I glanced in the rearview mirror at her, asking her if she had ever been on a plane before. "Nope, I never seen one, ever." Though I wasn't so happy about yelling in a car, I was pleased that she could have this new experience.

We met Kelly and Brody at the escalator with the hundreds of other people waiting for their friends and family members. The Atlanta Airport is a crowded one, and Kelly did not see us at first, save for Kolby and Jace crying out for their mother when they first spotted her. Kelly melted into my arms, completely done in and weary from her thirty two hour trip. As my lips covered her soft cheeks with kisses, Kolby and Jace threw their arms around her face. I picked up little Brody, who was dead on his feet from exhaustion, and was asleep in my arms before I could get his name out. The trip to Australia was, as always, a long and brutal one.

"Hi, mommy." Following our two girls' lead, Sydney hugged Kelly, as well.

"Hi," Kelly said, feebly. She shot me a questioning half smile. "You must be Sydney," she softly said.

"I'll fill you in later," I said, picking up the two fatigued travelers' carry on suit cases. My family had returned after a long separation. Little did Kelly know that when she returned, she would be mother to one more child.

CHAPTER 4

The weekend we were to have Sydney stay with us turned into weeks, and then months. A normal routine set in with Sydney as our fourth child. Now we had a child in kindergarten, first, and second grade, while Brody stayed home with Kelly. Kelly had been working on all of our children with reading and writing skills on a daily basis, as she stayed at home with them during the days, and either she or I read to the children a story each night. As a result, Kolby was becoming a good reader, and Jace was able to recognize all the letters of the alphabet, and even write her name. We quickly found out that Sydney could do none of this. This young girl, a little older than Kolby, could not read a word, recognize any letters, nor write her name. Kelly and I were careful to divide our attention between all four of the children with their skills, though Sydney needed extra attention.

She was also having problems in school with her behavior. While at home, Sydney always did what we asked her to, though she would often argue and fight with Brody, picking on him, as well. Jace and Kolby didn't seem to have this problem, perhaps because they were the same age, or same maturity level, roughly, and didn't take any gruff from her. Brody, though, was four years old, by this point, and still very much a toddler, our baby boy, as Kelly called him. When I would discipline Sydney, by having her stand in the corner, or take dessert away from her, she would not give me any problems in this area. School, though, was becoming another issue, we quickly found out.

The primary school where the girls went has a card system for its discipline procedure. Each day, every student begins at the green card level. If a child misbehaves and is disciplined by the teacher, the student places a yellow card by the name, which represents a warning. Yellow is followed by blue, which is a parental conference, and then by a red card, which is a conference with a school administrator. Our girls never "pulled a card," probably because they were too afraid of the consequences they would face at home. Sydney didn't seem to share this same concern, it appeared. The first few weeks went just fine with her, as she settled in. Yet, when she began to feel comfortable and relaxed in our house, Sydney had other ideas about school.

"Boom, Sydney had a problem at school today," Kelly said, meeting me in the yard, as I walked up the driveway after school.

"Again?" I asked. Sydney had been "pulling" a yellow card on average two to three times a week, mainly for not staying in her seat, and for excessive talking. We had tried a number of disciplinary matters with her; sent her to her to room after school, taken away privileges, no television. Apparently, none of them were working. "What did she do this time?" I was exasperated.

"She pulled a blue card," Kelly said. "Her teacher wrote in her school agenda that she continued to talk, even though she had been warned many times. I spoke with her teacher on the phone, and she said that Sydney is wild in class. I've already handled it; she's in her room right now."

A pattern was developing; Sydney would often misbehave in school the day after a visitation. Sydney's mother had been coming down from Atlanta to meet with Sydney during visitation. Sydney's mom was regularly on drugs, and had very little contact with her own mother, Sydney's grandmother, except during the visitation sessions. DFCS's policy is that a parent must have a drug check, if suspected of being under the influence, and there were those occasions when Sydney's mother either failed the test, or simply did not show up for the visitations. These were especially hard on the sad little seven year old girl. As I was often the one to pick her up on my way home from school each week, I was faced with the question of what to tell this young and confused girl why her mommy wasn't coming to see her. Too many times, I would walk into the DFCS visitation room, and find Sydney staring out the window, waiting for her mother to visit, with tears streaming down her face. Each time, my own heart would be filled with sadness; sadness for this little girl who was torn away from the only family she knew and placed with us, strangers in a strange home. "Why didn't my mommy come?" Sydney would ask me, between sobs.

"Sweetheart, maybe she's sick," I might answer one week. Another week, when faced with the same question, I would answer her with "Sydney, maybe her car is not working." How could I explain to a seven year old girl that her mother failed a drug test, or simply didn't show up? It wasn't fair to Sydney, and I came to feel anger towards her mother.

The weeks that Sydney's mother did show up were even harder, harder on us, that is. Sydney's mother would fill her daughter's mind with lies about us, much like Sarah and Mary Sue's mother would. Sydney would also be filled with sugary foods and drinks, resulting in a very high strung and agitated girl when she came home to us that evening. Usually, these evenings ended with Sydney yelling at Brody, screaming at Kelly and me, and simply upsetting the entire house, making for long nights. The nights that Sydney's grandmother visited, which were quite rare as she seldom came, were slightly better, but only slightly. Either way, visitation days were ones that we came to dread.

"ARGH! I hate lice!" Kelly was combing lice out of Sydney's hair, after washing her hair with a lice killing shampoo. I was never really a fan of lice, either, recalling the terrible time we had when Jace came down with it, years ago, while at a friend's house. It was very difficult to get out. "Where do you think she got it from?" my gloved wife asked me.

"Geez, hon, I don't know," I said, shrugging my shoulders.

"Well, I've had enough. It's your turn," she answered, handing me the comb. I smiled at her, or maybe it was a grin of suppression. I hated this job. Combing lice out of a child's hair was difficult and tedious. Not only did I have difficulty seeing the lice, Sydney was also high strung from her visit the day before with her grandmother, and was bouncing around on the chair. The last thing we wanted was to have Sydney pass the lice along to our own children. Besides, we wanted to get rid of the lice before we headed off to Disney World next week.

When Kelly was growing up in Australia, she spent a great deal of her time with many of her cousins, as the family was a tight-knit one. Gerard was one of these cousins, and as he was closest to Kelly in age, they basically grew up together, sharing many of the same experiences. Earlier this year, Gerard and his wife Leisa had moved to Philadelphia, PA, as Gerard was transferred in his military job for a three year stint. As we loved spending time with them, we took them to our favorite getaway, Disney World. Now, our own kids are spoiled when it comes to Disney World, as Kelly and I simply love the place. Perhaps love is too weak of a term. We are Disney Freaks, going any chance we can. This particular year, we decided to go camping at Disney's Fort Wilderness, a camping ground located in the theme park, itself. We traveled down the Friday before Thanksgiving and spent five days there, coming back the day before Thanksgiving Day. As Sydney was part of our family now, it seemed only natural that she came with us.

"I'm afraid that Sydney's mom said that she can't go with you," her caseworker, Barbara, told me over the phone.

"Why not?" I asked. I was shocked. DFCS has a policy that foster children are not allowed to travel over state lines without permission of the birth parents, which I completely understand. Surely, I thought, that the mother would allow us to take her child to Disney World. After all, this is the Magic Kingdom, every child's, as well as a few parents', dream vacation.

"She says she wants to take Sydney there, herself," Barbara responded.

"You're kidding!"

"I'm afraid not. In fact, her mom says that Sydney doesn't really want to go to Disney with you, and that you and Kelly are just putting that idea into Sydney's head."

"She said that?" Sydney's mother had been fighting us tooth and nail pretty much every step of the way. I was used to this, as foster parents are often the bad guys in the minds of the birth parents. "Barbara, that is just not true. We want to take her, as we want to give her this experience. I would hate to leave her behind in another foster home while we are gone, and have her miss it. Besides, how will she feel when we get back, and our kids are talking about it and showing her pictures? This is really going to hurt her." I was beginning to be adamant about this. "Here, please ask Sydney yourself if she wants to go." I gave Sydney the phone and sat back, infuriated. I really wanted Sydney to go, as I thought this might be her only opportunity for her to visit Disney as a child.

I heard Barbara ask Sydney over the phone if she wanted to go to Disney World with us. "Yes please! Yes please! Please let me go with Mommy and Daddy!" Sydney pleaded, jumping up and down as she spoke. It was pretty clear to me that she wanted to go.

Sydney gave the phone back to me. "Okay, I'll let the mother know that Sydney wants to go, and I'll ask her again. I'll let you know, John," Barbara said.

Two weeks later, we were all at Disney World, Sydney included. Her mother had changed her mind, and allowed her daughter to travel with us, after a deal of paperwork for DFCS. As always, our trip was great, and our family really gets the most out of our time at the Magic Kingdom. We slept in tents, and each morning, at sunrise, I would cook eggs, bacon, and pancakes. After that, we would hit the four parks, spending most of our time at the Magic Kingdom, itself. As Kelly and I are the biggest fans of Disney, we stayed out late each night, making sure we saw the fireworks whenever possible. When we did make it back to the campsite, it was late, and the kids were exhausted. Heck, I was tired, myself. Gerard and Leisa were excellent, and helped out whenever and where ever they could with the kids. Poor little Brody, it was only his second time at the parks, and his four year old legs soon gave out each day, prompting Gerard or I to carry him. By the time Wednesday morning came around, I was happy to pack up the tents and head back home. Thanksgiving was the next day, and even though it wasn't a day that Kelly celebrated in Australia, she had embraced my country's traditions on this day, and cooked a celebrated meal that was immensely tasty. Besides, we were going to spend this Thanksgiving with Gerard and Leisa, which we were all looking forward to.

Kelly had always been concerned with what we ate as a family. Good, healthy nutrition was important to her. I, on the other hand, enjoyed pizza, cheeseburgers, chocolate chip cookies, and, when the kids weren't looking, a good bowl of Fruity Pebbles. With three young children in the house, I would often sneak into my bedroom closet and chow down on a bowl of those delicious, colorful Pebbles, or eat my favorite ice cream flavor of the week. Nutrition wasn't my thing, though I was starting to come around. Slowly, I might add; real slow. Slow as in being dragged while resisting with all my sweet toothed might. I loved my chocolate chip cookies and my Fruity Pebbles almost as much as I loved Michigan State sports.

One night, after we had put the kids to bed for the night, Kelly and I sat down for some devotional time together. After some prayers, Kelly looked over at me. I could see that she was hesitating, wondering how to broach whatever subject she had on her mind.

"Boomie, I think that one of the reasons Sydney is so wild lately is because of her medication." DFCS had insisted that Sydney start taking medication for her ADHD, medication that her grandmother had given her. Initially, when Sydney came to live with us, there was not any medicine to give her, as DFCS wasn't aware of it. Two months ago, however, Sydney's grandmother mentioned to Barbara that Sydney was to take pills each day for the ADHD. I, too, had noticed that Sydney seemed a bit more "wild," though I wasn't sure why.

"So, that might explain why she was standing on the sink in the bathroom yesterday," I said. Sydney's teacher called me at work yesterday to inform me that she found Sydney hollering at the top of her lungs in the bathroom, while standing on the sink. I was able to get off work a little early, and met with the school's principal, along with Sydney, to discuss her recent behavior. The meeting wasn't pleasant for any of us, and the principal laid down the law with her. "What do you suggest?" I asked Kelly. I was running out of ideas, myself.

"Well, I've talked with Shannon, and she is okay with us taking Sydney off her medicine, and going with a healthy alternative. No junk food, no processed food, just healthy and organic food. I think it might be the best for her. At least, I want to give it a try. What do you think?" Shannon was not only one of our town's doctors, but Kelly's good friend. If Kelly and Shannon both agreed that this was a route that they might want to try with Sydney, than that was certainly good enough with me, and I told Kelly as much.

We started noticing a change shortly before Christmas. Sydney started to sleep better at night, and her behavior in school improved as well. She still had a tendency to lie, though, and we continued to work with her on trying to fix that. We battled another round of lice with her, making sure that it didn't spread through the house. It was around this time that Sydney's mother made another demand on us. She wanted to give Sydney a gift for Christmas; a gift that didn't sit well with us.

"Sydney's mother wants to give Sydney a new TV with a DVD player built into it, and wants you to allow Sydney to keep it in her room so she can watch TV whenever she wants," Barbara said, in her cold and emotionless manner, over the phone one night.

"Absolutely not!" I was firm in this, and was going to stand my ground. "My own children don't have a TV in their room. Why in the world would I allow Sydney to have one in her room?"

"The mother is insisting that she have one in her room, Mr. DeGarmo, and she's upset that you won't allow her daughter watch TV at night."

"Barbara, Kelly and I only allow our children to watch one movie a week. We are very careful about what our children watch on television, and do so because we are concerned." I was not going to back down on this. Kelly and I felt that there were a lot of negative and harmful images and shows on TV that are not appropriate for our young children, including Sydney.

"Well, I'll let her know, Mr. DeGarmo, but would you think it over, please? The mother would really like to do this for Sydney for Christmas," repeated the caseworker.

"I'm sorry, Barbara, but I am not going to allow Sydney to have a TV and DVD player in her bedroom. Not while she's living with us in our house." I felt bad for sounding so rude, but I felt strongly about this. Besides, I was growing a little weary of dealing with a mother who doesn't even show up half the time to see her own daughter. "Darn it," I thought after the phone call ended, "this is not a Christian attitude I am having towards the mother. She is a child of God, and Jesus loves her just as much as He loves me. I need to do better on this." I was struggling with my attitude here.

Christmas day was magical. It always is. It is the best day; the most special day of the year. And in our house, Kelly and I have created some wonderful traditions that make the day all the more magical. This year, we celebrated it with four children, and the house was full of excitement. Kelly's mother, Shirley, had come from Australia to join us that year, making it all the more special. Leading up to Christmas, we had been busy with many of the holiday festivities our town celebrates. I had once again sung in the town's Community Christmas concert, and our family joined many others in our church for an evening of Christmas caroling, followed by cookies and hot chocolate. The kids and I also did some Christmas caroling around our own neighborhood one afternoon, right before Christmas day. Kelly had helped Kolby and Jace bake homemade Christmas cookies, and we delivered some of these to our neighbors, spreading some good will and cheer of the season. We attended our church's Christmas Eve service, where I quite nervously sang "O Holy Night" to a gathering of very attentive friends and fellow church members. My knees shook the entire time, as sweat dribbled down the back of my neck. Even though I have sung and performed in front of thousands, I still become very nervous singing in front of friends and family in small gatherings.

As we were driving home from church that night, I pointed out to the four children the tiny red light silently jetting across the starry sky. "Children, do you see that red light up in the sky? Do you suppose that might be Rudolph?" Well, that did it. The silence of the night was ripped open by the sounds of four excited and thrilled children.

After all, Santa Claus was coming to visit, and he was on his way. Kelly and I had to work over time to get all four of them asleep before we started our duties for that singular night.

"He came! He came! He came!" Jace joyfully shouted, "Wake up, Kolby! Brody, Sydney, get up!" Kelly shook me, as she swiftly flew out of bed, herself. She quickly got dressed, and then dashed downstairs to wake her mother. I glanced at the clock; 6:30 AM. I moaned, perhaps a little bit too loudly. I wanted more sleep. Somehow, I managed to roll out of bed, slip my clothes on, and made it to the lounge room, where our 13 foot Christmas tree was surrounded by presents. All four kids stood at the top of the stairs, looking over the landing, waiting for Kelly's signal to come down. She had to position herself just right, with her camera, in order to capture each child's reaction.

"Okay, darlings, come..." She needn't finish her sentence. Thump! Thump! Thump! Thump! Thump! I stood back, afraid of getting crushed beneath the rapid feet of four children determined to make it down the stairs in under a half second, flat. We then gathered together around the fireplace, and each opened up the stocking that Kelly had sewn with each person's name on it. Earlier in the month, Kelly had made one for Sydney, and now it was completely filled with gifts. After this, we took a break, as I made blueberry and chocolate chip pancakes, while the kids got a head start on filling their tummies with donuts. Any house rule on sugary processed food flies out the window on Christmas day.

Breakfast was over, and we headed back into the lounge room. Kelly read the story of Jesus' birth to the children, and we sang Happy Birthday to Him. Afterwards, I put on my Santa hat, and passed out the presents. Sydney never had any toys while living with her grandmother, not even a doll, so Kelly and I went overboard with her. Some of our dear friends from church, Lynne and Steve, also had volunteered a few weeks beforehand to be Sydney's foster grandparents, and had bought a large amount of gifts for Sydney, a true blessing for not only her, but for Kelly and I, as it helped us treat Sydney to a wonderful Christmas morning. Dolls, strollers, clothes, books, and the like; she had the gift market all sewn up, receiving the most presents that day. She was excited, and couldn't contain herself, as she was wound up like a top. It was Christmas, though, and we let her have her fill of it. God had certainly blessed our household, and I felt fortunate to be able to share those blessings with her.

CHAPTER 5

"Daddy, mommy was on fire today..." Kolby pronounced to me, as I got home from work that day. It was the first day back to school after Christmas vacation, Jan. 5, and it was also Jace's sixth birthday. When the two of us were first married, Kelly had begun the tradition of taking me breakfast in bed on my birthday, and I treated her to the same on her birthday. It was a great way to start off our own special days, and we soon began doing it for our own children when they were out of the crib and in their own beds.

"Yeah, Daddy, it was REAL scary!" Sydney said, as she came up to me to give a hug. Jace just sat at the dining table, looking considerably terrified.

"What?" I replied, in a voice of astonishment, looking towards Kelly for an answer.

"Oh, Boom, it was terrible," Shirley declared.

Kelly began to unravel a story that left me flabbergasted and one that was slightly scandalous, if it got out to DFCS. It wasn't the best image for foster parents to set themselves on fire in front of their foster children.

Kelly had woken Shirley, Kolby, Brody, and Sydney early, and they all helped to prepare Jace's birthday breakfast. A glass of juice, a bowl of her special birthday cereal of choice, Cookie Crisp, a wrapped birthday present, and a cupcake were placed on a tray. Kelly lit a candle and pressed it into the cupcake, and all five of them walked up the stairs, into Jace's room. As they entered into the room, singing "Happy Birthday," Jace sat up and propped herself onto a pillow, with a drowsy smile slowly spreading across her face. Kelly bent down and placed the tray onto Jace's lap, while the others gathered around her bed, all in their pajamas. Kelly began to feel rather warm, thinking it was the warmth from the bathrobe.

The joyful birthday tradition took a turn, as the cheery morning was abruptly shattered. "Mommy's on fire!" Sydney shrieked. Bedlam rapidly took over, as Brody and Kolby began to scream in panic. Kelly looked down, horrified to find her arm on fire. Her bathrobe was ablaze, lit from the candle that had brushed against her robed arm when she had bent over Jace. Shirley immediately began to beat against her own daughter, Kelly. Brody and Kolby fled from the room in terror. "I'll get a bucket of water!" Sydney yelled. Instead, she stood frozen in place, wide eyed, watching in horror, as the flames began to spread over Kelly's robe, unto her back. Jace sat in her bed, in trepidation.

"I moved across the room, praying the entire way, and took off the robe," Kelly said to me. I had to pick my jaw off the ground, as I was gaping in bewilderment. As the robe fell to the ground, ablaze, Shirley and Kelly began to stamp the fire out with their feet. Sydney stood nearby, crying. Jace remained in bed, quietly shaking. What a way to start off not only the day, but a birthday. On top of that, Kelly still had to restore calm to all of the children, get them dressed, and downstairs to breakfast. After all, she had to drop the kids off to school, and ready herself for a day's worth of massages. Calling Brody and Kolby back into the room, she gave each a quick hug, told them mommy was all right, and reassured Jace, who had yet to make a single sound through the entire experience. It was quite a birthday bash. She still had a present to open up, as well. Birthday breakfast in bed would never be quite the same.

"Not again!" Kelly cried out to me from the bathroom. She was giving Sydney a bath. I called out to her from the kitchen, asking her what was wrong, dreading the answer I might get. "She has lice again!" Darn it; that was the answer I was dreading. "This has got to stop," my wife demanded.

It was March, my favorite time of year, as college basketball entered into its March Madness tournament, with sixty four college teams across the US playing for a chance to win the National Championship. I cheered on my Michigan State University Spartans with a passionate fervor which my wife found bordered on mental instability, or at the least, simply crazy. Yet, it was also March madness in our home, as well. We seemed to be losing our battle with one of our dreaded enemies, lice. This was the third time Sydney had been re-infected with it, and we were doing all we could to keep it at bay from the rest of the family. Both Kelly and I had spent lengthy hours bent over Sydney's head, combing the lice out. Apparently, we needed another tactic.

I called Barbara the next day and informed her about Sydney, yet again. Kelly and I both come to the conclusion that her grandmother was re-infecting her, as Sydney only came down with it just after visitations with her. "It's the only reason I can come up with, Barbara. Our kids don't have it, no one at church has it, and she is not getting it from school," I told our caseworker over the phone. "We can't keep having her come home with lice each time. Sooner or later, it's going to spread through our house."

Barbara took a moment before she answered, as I heard her drum her fingers against a table. "Well, Mr. DeGarmo," she sighed. She would not call me by my first name, though I insisted upon it, time and time again. "We can have her grandmother checked for lice before each visit. We will have to tell her that she won't be able to visit her granddaughter if she, herself, has lice."

"Thanks, that will be a great help," I assured Barbara. "Otherwise, we are just going to have to give her a very short haircut."

"Oh, no, please don't do that, Mr. DeGarmo," Barbara quickly replied.

"Well, we just can't have her bringing lice back to our house, again," I declared to her.

As I hung up the phone, I recalled one of DFCS' policies of haircuts. Foster parents are not allowed to give foster children haircuts without permission and approval of the birth parents. I always felt that this rule was a ridiculous one. After all, foster parents did everything else for the child, often running ourselves ragged to do so, many times at our own expense. Yet, foster parents are not allowed to give a child a haircut. It boggled my mind. I was also well aware that Sydney's mother would not permit it, either.

Spring passed with its many colors and smells abounding. Forsythia bloomed, daffodils and tulips danced in the April and May breeze, hummingbirds returned to our feeders, and summer flowers began to poke their heads out of the ground. Before we knew it, June was upon us, and that meant summer vacation for the kids and I. As a teacher, I embraced it. Heck, I believe I enjoy summer vacation more than most of my students. The big kid in me, I suppose.

The three girls attended various vacation Bible school summer camps throughout town. Brody learned how to swim at the public pool. Sydney learned, too, as she was never taught. She also learned how to ride a bike, as I taught both her and Jace at one of the nearby church parking lots. Our driveway consisted mainly of a very steep hill, and was only sanctioned for professional daredevils and stunt performers. No bike riding lessons at our place. It was a long summer, and a wonderful summer. It was also the start of a new adventure for me; I was going back to school.

Kelly had been mentioning to me for a couple of years about becoming a school media specialist, which is the new, twenty-first century term for school librarian. For two years, I had brushed off her suggestion, completely content within the classroom. I enjoyed being a teacher. I relished the opportunity to not only teach the children, but to entertain them at the same time. I was a firm believer that students, young and old, needed to enjoy the learning process. Otherwise, if the student lacked interest in the topic, learning suffers, and ceases altogether.

My classroom became, at times, my stage, as I performed and entertained for them as they learned about poetry, Shakespeare, and even grammar. I put a large amount of effort into my portrayal of the great Shakespeare play, Romeo and Juliet, for my ninth graders each year, trying to bring the 500 year old play to life and making it relevant for the students, as I performed the entire play singlehandedly for the class, my audience. Weekly spelling quizzes became opportunities for me to work on my voice impressions, as I presented each word to be spelled in different accents. Even grammar lessons became entertaining, as I used puppets and other forms of drama, solely intended to keep the interest of the students, as they learned these important building blocks of the English language.

Yet, at the same time, I was feeling like it was time to move on. Perhaps God had other plans for me. Kelly had heard that one of the media specialists in our county's school system was planning to retire in the next year, and she thought that it might be a great job for me. I had been offered an English teaching position in our small town a few years back, but I didn't accept it, as I felt my place was elsewhere. Now, I was feeling called back to our home, back to our small town and to our community. The people of Monticello had opened up their arms and embraced a "Yankee" and a "Foreigner," as Kelly and I were often referred to, in a humorous way. It seemed that whenever I introduced myself in Monticello, I would get the same response, "Oh, you must be married to Kelly, from Australia." My bride had certainly made a name for herself in the short time we lived here, and I was happy for her. As I worked out of town, I did not know many people outside of church activities. Certainly working in Monticello would change that, and I looked forward to this. Kelly also was anxious for me to work in our town's school system, as I would be able to be there for our own children. Maybe being a media specialist in our town would save me from the concerns I had, yet at the same time, allow me to give back to the community that had given so much to us.

After a great deal of prayer, I made the decision to go back to college and earn my master's degree in Media Technology. It was a two year course, and I was rather nervous, and a little apprehensive about it. After all, I hadn't been in a classroom as a student in twenty odd years. Sure, I read and graded thousands of essays as an English teacher, but I wasn't so sure I was ready to write them. Even more than that, I was not one who had happily embraced technology, and didn't know much beyond turning a computer on and off. How was I going to do in a Media Technology course? Yet, I took the plunge, and began the journey of finally gaining a master's degree.

Summer came to an end. Our weekly trips to the Plant Parlor for ice cream cones had to wait for another year. Swim suits were stored away for next summer. Days spent in the garden had come and gone. All these had to wait for next summer. School was back in session, and that meant four children this year. Brody was starting kindergarten. It also meant Kolby was to begin her own adventure at a new school, too, as she started third grade at the elementary school. We now had a child in kindergarten, first, second, and third grade. The DeGarmo children were invading the school system.

The end of summer also meant that Sydney had been with us for just less than one year. We had grown to very much love her, as she was part of our family. Her reading and writing skills had come a long way, and her behavior was also improving a great deal, as well. Yet, her future was uncertain, as her mother was not making the progress nor taking the steps she needed with DFCS in order to keep custody of her daughter. Kelly and I were very concerned, yet we weren't getting the answers from DFCS about Sydney's future, simply because DFCS didn't know, either. A meeting was called with Sydney's mother, grandmother, a DFCS evaluator, and myself in order to determine the next course of action. It wasn't a pleasant meeting.

Arriving after work to the meeting, I entered into the DFCS building a little uneasy. I had not met either of Sydney's relatives. Following Sue, the evaluator's lead, I entered the small meeting room on the second floor of the DFCS building. It was a dark room, with many shadows, lit by a sole overhead light. Already seated at the wooden table was Sydney's grandmother, whom I instantly recognized by the picture pillow Sydney slept with each night. She looked gaunt and worn-down, just like she did in the picture. Seated next to her was another worn and haggard looking lady, though younger in appearance. Before seating myself in one of the two chairs opposite the table from the two, I introduced myself, extending my hand in greeting. Sydney's grandmother took it and introduced herself as Kate, with a weak smile. The other person simply sat there, with a scowl on her face, and chose not to shake hands. This already isn't going very well, I thought to myself.

After I was seated, the evaluator introduced the others across from me. It was indeed Sydney's mother, looking like she would be anywhere in the world except where she was at that moment, across the table from the foster parent who was caring for her daughter. I understood and appreciated how she felt, but I felt uncomfortable, too. This wasn't easy for either of us, though much harder for her.

The evaluator led us through the file on Sydney, and detailed how Kelly and I had made progress with Sydney with her reading and writing, as well as school work in general. She also explained to both of Sydney's family members the growing relationship that Sydney had with our own three children, and how Sydney had come to take a lot more responsibility for her actions in our home. Kate looked at me. "I want to thank ya, Mr. DeGarmo, for all you and yur wife are doin' with Sydney. I can see that she's learned a lot."

"Thank you very much," I replied. "We very much enjoy having Sydney with us."

"And she likes stayin' with ya," she said. "I'm getting my stuff t'gethuh, and I'm thinkin' that she'll be able to cum and live with me real soon. I know my daughta's been wurking real hurd, too." Her eyes were thick and filmy. Her voice, thick with accent, was tainted by the stark smell of alcohol.

I had been studying Sydney's mother throughout the meeting, and had noticed she had been agitated since the moment it began, but I wasn't prepared for what happened next. " 'Scuse me," she announced, "Sydney tells me that y'all make her do chores 'round y'alls house."

Her voice held venom in it, her eyes flaring with fury. I knew that I had to tread carefully. "Yes, ma'am, we do." Since coming to the Deep South, I had learned the importance of the word "ma'am, and the respect it dignified. It was a word I never used while growing up in Michigan, but I had quickly adapted it once moving to Monticello. I recognized that now was a perfect time to use it.

"Well, that aint right. She shouldn't be doing no chores for y'all!"

"Ma'am, all of my children do chores in my house, as we feel that it teaches them responsibility," I said, calmly.

"Well," she paused, "Sydney says that you make her feed the cat every day. I don't think she should have to feed the cat ev'ry single day."

I took a breath, hesitated, and then responded. "Actually, the children all take turns feeding the cat. Sydney only feeds it once a week, every Wednesday, while the other three children feed it twice a week."

"I don't want my daughtur feedin' yur cat!" she demanded.

"I'm sorry, ma'am, but Sydney is going to have chores as long as she is living with us." I might have been wrong, but I felt that this was only best for Sydney, as it not only taught her personal responsibility, but it also helped make her feel like one of the family.

Unfortunately, Sydney's mother wasn't done with me just yet. She lurched over the table, thrusting her finger in my face. "Do you wash her hair?"

"Um....pardon me?" Where was this leading?

"Do YOU wash her hair?" she challenged.

"Yes, ma'am, I do." Was this a problem?

"Well, the las' time I saw her, her hair wuz dirty," she said, frowning.

"I'm sorry." The words sounded silly to me, but I didn't know what else to say.

"I don't WANT you washing her hair! It aint right."

I thought for myself about how best to answer this before replying. "Ma,am, the nights my wife is at work, I bathe all three girls together, and wash their hair at the same time. Of course, when Sydney has had lice, we have to wash her hair separately, with some lice killing shampoo." Fortunately, since DFCS had begun testing Kate for lice, we had been spared of a fourth infestation. Sydney's mother wasn't satisfied, though, as she leapt from her chair, grabbing a piece of paper in front of her, rolling it into a ball, and threw it at me. But, she was just getting started, as she began to spew forth a tirade laced with profanity, calling me every name in the book, and then some I had never heard before. Kate tried to restrain her, telling her to sit down, but the mother would not listen. I sat there, stunned, feeling trapped. Where could I go? I began to pray 1 Corinthians 13: 4 over and over in my mind. "Love is patient, love is kind. Love is patient, love is kind. Love is PATIENT! Love is KIND!"

And then, she spat on me.

I didn't say anything, just wiped the spittle off my face, and looked towards the evaluator. Obviously, this had gotten out of control. Before Sue could say anything, Sydney's mother shoved her chair in, yelling, "I aint stayin' for this!" storming out, and slamming the door behind her, in a fit of rage. There was momentary silence in the room, tension weighing heavily in the air, as no one knew how to react.

After the brief pause, Kate told the two of us, "I'm sorry 'bout her. If ya 'scuse me, please, ah guess ah should check on my daughtur." I shook my head yes, still a little rattled, while the evaluator joined her in the hall. Time stood still. The clock's ticking was deafening to me. How long am I supposed to sit here, I wondered.

A few moments went by. Five minutes. Ten minutes. Then, the door opened, and Sue walked in, followed by Kate. As they sat down at the table, Sue apologized to me, and informed me that these types of meetings don't normally go this way. That didn't seem to comfort me any, as I wasn't particularly thrilled that I could be the one to break that cycle. Kate would not return my eye contact, as I tried to reassure her with a smile that all was fine. Sue continued, as she informed me that she believed Sydney's mother was lashing out from stress, as she was told earlier today that DFCS would be asking the judge to sever her rights with her daughter, Sydney. Ah.... It made sense. Sydney's mom was not only angry, she must have feelings of guilt, I surmised. I also imagined that she was embarrassed in front of me. I held no hard feelings, and told both Kate and Sue that. Sue finished by saying that DFCS was investigating an aunt and uncle in Florida, who had expressed some interest in taking Sydney into their home.

As I left DFCS that day, I wasn't really sure how I felt. Sure, I was still bowled over by Sydney's mother and her actions toward me. I was also feeling a little stunned about Sue's comments about Sydney's aunt and uncle. What did that really mean? Were these good people? Would it be a good, loving, stable home? Would it be a Christian home, something I had been praying for? And most puzzling, how much longer would Sydney be with us?

Shortly after this, Kelly had a scare herself. One afternoon after school, Kelly and the four kids were shopping for groceries at the local grocery store. It has been a tiring day at work for Kelly, and she was anxious to get home and start dinner. The three girls had homework to do, as well. It was the normal routine, or so Kelly thought. Normalcy for a foster parent takes different forms, as she was about to be reminded.

The grocery cart was already full as Kelly pushed it down the frozen food aisle. Brody was fidgeting in the seat, in front of Kelly, while Kolby, Jace, and Sydney were following close behind. The three girls were each offering their mother suggestions to add on to an ever growing grocery bill, as kids often do. Each suggestion was voiced in their little voices in earnest. As Kelly patiently listened to each suggestion, she noticed, out of the corner of her eye, a couple staring at them from the other end of the aisle. Monticello is a small town, and a trip to the grocery store often turns into a gathering of friends and family. This couple, though, were strangers to her.

She wheeled the cart into the next lane, thinking it must be her imagination. The girls were letting Kelly know they were hungry, missing their after school snack. As Kelly headed up the lane, the couple reappeared on the far side. They were clearly staring at them, Kelly determined. An older couple, perhaps in their fifties or sixties, as both male and female were grey and wrinkled with age. They were clad in dirt covered and faded clothing, Kelly observed, and were very focused on the five of them. The female waved at Sydney, and the eight year old waved back at her. Do they know her, Kelly wondered to herself. She grabbed some frozen spinach from the freezer, quickly turning the cart around and headed to the checkout counter.

As the Australian pushed the cart laden with groceries to the car, the older couple soon exited the store, and headed towards Kelly's car. Hustling the children into the car with one hand as quickly as she could, and the food in the other hand, Kelly turned to face the couple as they were walking towards her. Remembering my experience with Sydney's mother a few weeks back, she was concerned this pair might be friends of hers, seeking some sort of revenge, and settling some score. Bracing herself, the mother of four smiled bravely, trying not to stumble over words that were caught in her throat. "May I help you with something?" She placed herself between the children, who were watching intently, and the strange pair, waiting; waiting for what, she did not know.

"Hi. ah'm Melissa, and this here is my husband Jake." The elderly lady extended her hand in greeting to Kelly, who took it. Kelly began to relax her vigil a little as the elderly lady continued. "We know Sydney, and ah wanted to meet ya and tell ya thankya for all y'all are doin' for her. Ya see, it was us that reported her ta DFCS. We live next door ta Sydney's granmah. Sydney use ta call out ta us from her bedroom winda ev'ry day. She'd justa sit there, up in her bedroom, and look out it. When she'd see us, she'd call out to us, and ask us fer food. She'd be real hungry, she'd say. Ev'ry day, it'd be like that. It weren't a good home fer her. And her granmah couldn't take care of her, nohow. So, we just called up DFCS one mornin', after she went ta school, and told them 'bout her."

Kelly wasn't sure what to say. This was certainly not what she had expected when the couple first approached her. Not after what happened with Kayla and Patty Sue's parents in the parking lot one afternoon. "G'day. I'm Kelly," she said, with her thick Australian accent and warm smile unfolding across her face. "It's very nice to meet you."

"Thank ya," Melissa said, as Jake stood next to her, smiling. "She looks so good," Melissa continued, indicating towards Sydney, "and ah just wanted to say hello to her. Ah can tell that she's in a good home. Thank ya for takin' care of her. We're real fond of her."

As Kelly drove off, afterwards, she played over the conversation again in her head. "Dear God," she prayed silently to herself, "thank You for Melissa and Jake. Thank You that they contacted DFCS for Sydney. Thank You, Lord, that my children are all safe, and that all are well. Jesus, I pray that You bless Melissa and Jake, and that You hold them in Your hand, watching over them. Please help us help Sydney, too, God. I love You, Lord. Amen."

We received word shortly before we were to head to Disney World that Sydney would not be able to travel with us. As we had the past few years, we would head down there on the Friday before Thanksgiving, and return the Wednesday before the Great Day of Food; Thanksgiving. This year, she would be spending it with an aunt and an uncle in Florida. Barbara had called to tell us that Sydney would be leaving us soon to go and live with them. Our whole family was stunned. Sydney had been with us for almost a year and a half by that point, and was very much a sibling to our own three children, and had become dear to Kelly and myself. I knew that I was supposed to be happy for her that she would have a true family to live with, but I had difficulty mustering up those feelings of happiness. Instead, I was sad that she would be leaving us soon. But, more than that, I was worried for her. Is this the right place for her? Will she find it a home where she is loved, taught, and even raised by Christian family members? I had many discussions with Barbara about it, expressing my concerns, and becoming frustrated that there were no answers forthcoming.

Kelly spoke with the aunt before heading off to Disney, and received instructions on where we could drop her off, as they lived on our way to the Magic Kingdom. Afterwards, Kelly handed the phone to Sydney, and the two became acquainted. At least, as acquainted as an 8 year old can be over the phone with an adult that she had never met. Kelly then ended the conversation explaining to the aunt about Sydney's diet, daily schedule, and other needs. Days later, we met the aunt at a store nearby her house, her husband being at work. Sydney seemed nervous about going with her, and was disappointed that she couldn't join us at Disney. Sure, what child wouldn't want to go see Mickey and his friends, I thought. I was uncomfortable with the whole situation, but it was very much out of my hands, as Kelly had to remind me. I wasn't in charge of Sydney; she wasn't my child. I had to begin to let go of her in my life and in my heart.

After Thanksgiving, we began to receive weekly calls from the aunt and uncle. They had a younger son, a four year old boy, and seemed eager to have Sydney come and live with them. I had to restrain myself from asking too many questions, though it was hard. I felt like a mama grizzly bear protecting her young. Kelly and I were told to expect Sydney moving shortly after Christmas, and we prepared our children for it. "Daddy, will she come and visit us in the summer?" Brody wanted to know.

"That sounds like a great idea," Kelly said, patting our son on the shoulder.

Like the year before, Sydney had the largest amount of presents under the thirteen foot tree that Brody and I had cut down. Lynne and Steve once more blessed our family, as they again served as Sydney's adoptive foster grandparents, buying her many gifts. The tree was full of presents, the house was utterly adorned for Christmas from top to bottom, and the excitement of the day was overflowing in our house. Soon, it would be Christmas day!

I answered the phone late December 22, and the moment I heard Barbara's detached and emotionless voice, I knew in my gut that a gloomy pale would soon envelope our home. "Mr. DeGarmo, the aunt and uncle will be coming from Florida tomorrow to take Sydney home with them. They want to have her with them before Christmas."

I was floored. Really? Right before Christmas? "Barbara, do you think it's a good idea for Sydney to go and spend Christmas day with strangers? She's been with us for a year and a half, her stocking is full, there are presents under the tree for her, and the kids are all excited. I wonder if this is best for her. Can't it wait until at least December 26?" I was pleading.

"No, the family wants her for Christmas. They are staying the night in Macon, and will be at DFCS at nine in the morning. Can you meet them there?"

I didn't know what to say. I heard myself mutter "Sure," and distantly heard Barbara say she would let the family from Florida know that we would be there before hanging up. It was wrong, I felt. But, there was nothing I could do. I went into the bedroom, where I found Kelly wrapping some last minute presents, and broke the news to her. Like me, she was upset. I sat down next to her, taking her hand, and led the two of us in prayer; prayers for us and a prayer for Sydney, thanking God for her in our lives and asking Him to bless her on her new journey.

It was a cold, damp morning as I stood outside DFCS the next day. The wind was blowing, and there were grey clouds lingering in the sky. Kelly and the kids had bid their tearful goodbyes to Sydney at home, while I had packed the van with all of her belongings, plus the bounty of wrapped Christmas presents. Now, it was my turn to say goodbye. After placing all of her belongings into her uncle's truck, I knelt down besides her and took her small hands in mine. As I looked into her eyes one last time, I could see that she was confused, yet excited at the same time. I asked the aunt and uncle to join us in prayer. After thanking God for Sydney and asking Him to bless her, I gave her one last hug, and told her I loved her, tears spilling down my cheeks. I then watched her enter the truck, and waved goodbye. After a year and a half in our lives, and in our home, I hoped that this wasn't the last time I would see her.

CHAPTER 6

We were tired and we needed a break. Kelly and I came to the same conclusion, we found, as we went out to dinner one night in February. It had been roughly a month and a half since Sydney had left to go live with her aunt and uncle, and we were spending our first night out together without children in a very, very long time. DFCS has many rules and restrictions in regards to having a baby sitter when a foster child is in the house, and this was our first time away from home in the year and a half that Sydney came to live with us. We desperately needed this night together, if simply to sit across the table from each other and have an adult conversation, away from home, and away from any children.

We missed her. The house was a little quieter without her. I missed hearing her call me Daddy. Yet, at the same time, our family had suffered a little with Sydney in the house. We both felt that our own children had been somewhat neglected by us as we focused so much attention on Sydney. Whether it was helping her with her weak school skills, her discipline, or her habit to lie, she had left us drained. Poor Brody had taken the brunt of it, as those two were often fighting about one thing or another. It was Kelly who suggested we take some time off from fostering, at least until we recharged our batteries, and more importantly, focus on our own children.

Kelly's business was growing. The place she was renting from no longer could accommodate her, and soon she found herself looking for another place to work out of. We both put this to prayer, and by the end of the school year, Kelly had bought an old house in town, and moved her business there. Fortunately, her business only benefitted from it, as she had more clients than she could have ever hoped for. God, though, had other plans for her.

Nutrition and good health had long been a concern as well as an interest of Kelly's. After a great deal of thought, Kelly approached me about going back to school, herself, in order to earn a doctorate in nutrition, a Naturopathic doctor. We prayed about it, discussed it, and prayed about it again. It would be a big step, a big commitment for both of us. I was half way through my master's program. Two adults working full time and enrolled in school would only add to the work load in our house. Plus the added pressure of Kelly owning her own business was taxing, as well. We needed a season off from being foster parents.

Summer was filled with the usual; gardening, swimming, bike riding, and the simplicity of children at play. Kolby went to church choir camp that summer, as well. Before we knew it, summer was over. I entered into the new school year, 2006-2007, with the knowledge that this would probably be my last one at the school. It was my tenth year there, and they were good years, though God's call to work in Monticello was growing stronger and stronger in my ear each day. I was pleased to see that my master's courses were easier than I first anticipated, and I was enjoying them, as well. That fall, the writing bug bit me, too. I had always enjoyed the writing process outside of the classroom. My love of gardening also was growing, and it made sense to join the two together, I surmised. I approached the town newspaper about writing a gardening column. To my pleasant surprise, they were more than happy to publish it. The newspaper is published once a week and my column saw publication every two weeks.

In the fall, I began to have a change of heart. At the back of my brain was the persistent voice that told me that I needed to be fostering children. Neal, my friend and fellow teacher, would often question why I wanted to do it. "You're too busy," he would say, fearing I would burn myself out. My family had a similar view. Yet, I couldn't shake the feeling, and told Kelly as much. Was God calling us again to foster? It was hard with Sydney, and it was also hard with her moving. We continued to pray for her, as well as Sarah and Mary Sue, despite not having any idea of their wellbeing.

December 16th began like any other day. It was the last week of school before Christmas vacation, and that meant Final Exams for my classes. That week, the first three days were exam days for students, with the remaining Thursday and Friday scheduled as teacher work days, where teachers were able to grade exams, finalize semester grades, and the mountain of general paperwork that often escalates into an avalanche, enveloping a teacher. I was looking forward to the Christmas break, and I figured that this would be a rather light week of work for me, as the paperwork and grading are not hindrances to me. I figured wrong.

That afternoon, before I left home from work, Kelly called me let me know that she had received "the call." This time, DFCS had a baby, and wanted to know if we would take it. Now, like any loving mother, my wife adores babies. She had cherished her time with Mary Sue, and had often told me that she would enjoy fostering a newborn baby. We had come to the decision when we first started fostering that we would not take into our home foster children who were older than our own children. "Yes, we will," she told Nancy, the caseworker. Then she caught herself; "let me call my husband first, though, just to make sure."

My heart was racing as Kelly told me about the conversation over the phone. I asked the first question that came to my mind, "Is it a boy or a girl?" It had been one year since Sydney had left, and I was ready.

"I don't know. Let me find out some more information, and then call you back. But, let's pray about it first."

"Lord, it's been a year now, and we are unsure what You would have us do. Please open our eyes to what You would have us do with this little baby. Amen." It was a short prayer, as I stood in the school secretary's office, holding the phone in my hand. "Okay, just let me know, hon. Find out what we need to know, and then make a decision. I'll support whatever you decide to do, but I think we can do this." I had to get back to my classroom.

Bewildered, I returned to my students as Kelly called Nancy back. The caseworker informed Kelly that the baby girl was only five days old, and was of mixed race. The term was a new one to Kelly, and she was grateful when Nancy described to her that the baby, whose name was Mariah, had a "white" mother and a "black" father. In our household, we had raised our children not to refer to people as "black" or "white." I had always felt that the terms were divisive, as the words automatically place people into categories based on skin color. Since no human being is truly white, and that no human is truly black, we had taught our children that all people are the same color, just different shades of God's skin.

Nancy went on to tell Kelly some startling information about the baby. Mariah's mother had stumbled into the hospital in town five nights ago, looking for drugs of some kind. As the nurse of the tiny hospital spoke with the young mother, she noticed that the mother was not only under the influence of drugs, but was also pregnant and in labor. Mariah was born two months premature, weighing only five pounds. What was most disturbing, though, was that Mariah was what DFCS classified as a "crack baby," as her mother was on crack during her pregnancy. DFCS was not sure how Mariah would respond to the deadly drug in her system, and what the long terms effects might be, if any. Shocked by the mother's condition, as well as following policy, the hospital staff contacted DFCS, informing them of the potential harm to Mariah. Before the mother had much time to spend with her newborn daughter, DFCS swept in and took supervision of the newest and tiniest addition to Monticello.

The hospital is indeed a small one, and does not have a birthing unit. Babies birthing in Monticello was not a common practice; in fact, Mariah's birth there was big news, as it was the first baby born at the rural hospital in over a year. She was the talk of the hospital. After she was born, Mariah was transferred to another hospital an hour away, where she was placed on a breathing apparatus. It was on the fifth day that she came back to Monticello. After Kelly had spoken with Nancy a second time, she agreed to take Mariah in as a foster child, calling me back at school to let me know. It was 4:30 by the time I arrived back in town, at DFCS. Walking upstairs to the caseworker's office, I found Kelly there, and in her arms lie the tiniest baby I had ever laid eyes upon. She was wrapped in a paper dress, as neither the hospital nor DFCS had any clothes small enough to fit her. Her brown, curly hair was thick, and her skin was a deep brown color. Kelly placed her in my arms, and I became quickly astonished that a human being could fit into my hand. The baby was small and light enough to fit into a single hand of mine. Though I had held babies many times in my arms, I held this one cautiously, as if the world depended on it. Perhaps it was the fact that she was helpless and a "crack baby"; perhaps it was because she was so tiny. Whatever the reason, I believe I fell in love with the tiny, vulnerable newborn child right then and there.

Our own kids met us at the door when we arrived home, anxious to peek at their new playmate. Kelly was quick to tell them, though, that five day newborns don't do much playing. Kolby and Jace each wanted to hold "Baby Mariah," as they soon christened her, while Brody stood at arm's length, as he closely examined the infant. Shirley had come over from Australia just days before. Gerard and Leisa were to join us, shortly, as well as Gerard's brother, Shaun. The house would soon be spilling over with joy and merriment during this most holy of seasons. Mariah was simply an early gift to our family.

After dinner, Kelly and I visited Lynne and Steve's house for a Christmas party, and many of our dear friends and members of the community were sure to be there. I was anxious to introduce our church family to their newest member, and proudly took the little cherub to their house. I felt like a proud father with the little bundle tucked securely into my arms. She was the talk of the party, and was instantly loved by our friends and church family.

The first night spent with Mariah was grueling, as the newborn screamed throughout the night, following the same pattern for the next two weeks. Kelly and I wearily took turns throughout the nights, trying to comfort her, as the drugs weaned out of her system. The days were a little easier, though, as we had plenty of arms who wished to hold and feed her. Kelly took off the next day, Tuesday, and stayed at home with her, though had to return to work on Wednesday, and for the rest of that week. Day care would not be available for her until after Christmas. After speaking with my school's principal, I was given permission to take Mariah to work with me on those last three days of the semester. As the students were on vacation, I was able to watch over her, grading papers and completing the necessary paperwork required for the semester's end as she lay in a portable crib in my classroom. Soon, word leaked out through the faculty members, who rushed out to buy the baby clothes that fit, diapers, and formula. Members of our church were rapidly doing the same. Kelly and I were deeply touched by the outreach and the general compassion of so many people; people intent on helping us out.

It was during Christmas vacation that Shaun came to fall in love with Mariah, as well. Gerard's thirty something brother had never been married nor had kids of his own, but he cared for Mariah as if she were his own, holding her in his arms whenever he could snatch her away from Kelly or one of the girls. What's more, the joke was that Mariah's head never touched a bed, as she was held constantly by anyone and everyone. DFCS, in truth, encouraged this, as Nancy told us to love the newborn with all we had, to smother her with compassion and care due to the trauma she suffered when first born. Yet, I was curious. Was everyone fawning over Mariah simply because we were encouraged to? Maybe it was because she was a foster child born into a tragic situation. Or was it something different? I wasn't certain, but I continued to dwell upon it. Nevertheless, it was another magical Christmas, filled with love, family, traditions, and the love of Christ abounding in our home, interrupted each night, though, by Mariah's drug weaning screams hammering away at my sleep. Ugh!

"Daddy, did you get our corsages?" Kolby's face was aglow with the excitement of the day, and fired the question at me as soon as I walked up the stairs. I handed her the package of the three flowers; two corsages and one boutonniere.

"They're beautiful," Kelly said, giving me a kiss, while attending to Jace's hair. Both girls were dressed to the T. Make up, hair, fancy evening gowns, nails done professionally. They were ready for the big night.

I had been looking forward to this night for a few months, now, ever since I read the article in a magazine about a church that held a Father/Daughter Dance. I had organized a similar event at our church, and asked a few of the dads to help me prepare. The dance was a way to honor our daughters and granddaughters as gifts from God, as well as to teach them that they are to be treated by men with respect, dignity, class, and integrity. I had been nervous throughout the day leading up to our first dance, hoping that all would be right; the dj, the food, the photos, and most importantly, the people, would enough show up? It had been a concern of mine for weeks, and I worked hard getting people excited during the weeks that led up to it.

"Let me get your picture beforehand," Kelly said, grabbing the camera off the shelf, and organizing the four of us. I was not only taking Jace and Kolby, but seven week old Mariah was to be the youngest dancer that night. With Kolby and Jace by my side, I held our foster baby in my arms, beaming with pride over my two girls plus one more.

The night was a sensation, successful beyond anything I anticipated. Kelly, along with many of the moms, was there at the beginning, cheering on all the young ladies. After a first dance, Kelly took Mariah home, and I danced the night away with my two princesses, kicking off my shoes along with the other dads, having the time of my life, and thanking God for the blessings in my life with daughters and dear friends by my side.

Three months into the new year of 2007, Mariah had wrapped her way into everyone's heart that came in contact with her. Yet, I continued to keep a wall up between us, not giving myself over to her entirely. I had felt much pain and grief over Sarah, Mary Sue, and Sydney, and there was no doubt in my mind that Mariah would be the toughest of all to handle, as she was with us since basically the day she was born. I refused to think of her as mine. Kelly and the kids on the other hand, well, they were head over heels.

Visitations with Mariah's mother were a little different than our previous experience. Her mother had been placed in jail two months after Mariah was born for trying to cash a bad check, as well as parole violation, which created a little bit of a problem for the visitation. Kelly and I were not about to travel four hours there and back simply to take the baby to see a mother she did not even know for an hour visit. The visits were during the weekdays, and Kelly and I were not able to take off the time from work. DFCS stepped in and hired a driver to take Mariah to the jail and back each week. Kelly and I were uncomfortable with this, as we felt a baby did not need to be taken to a jail to visit a stranger merely to satisfy the mother. Yet, as is often the case with being a foster parent, we had no say in the manner, and had to work alongside DFCS in this.

"Boomie, we need to be praying for the mother, as well," Kelly told me one night.

"I know, but it's hard for me sometimes," I admitted. Once again, I was struggling with the birth parents, as I was angry. How could people do such horrible things to little children? Why did I have to raise a child that was not my own? I felt called by God to do it, to be a foster parent, as the need was so strong, and so many unwilling to do it. But, I was angry that there was a need at all. I had a hard time looking at Kelly in the eye, as the guilt for my anger washed over me. "You're right," I answered, sighing aloud, "I'll start praying for her." I took her hand, as I led us in prayer. "Father God, I ask You to forgive my hardness of heart. Please bless Mariah's mother, and fill her heart with your presence.

Please bless Mariah, as well; granting us the wisdom and the grace totake care of her while she is with us. Thank You so much for Kolby, Jace, and Brody, who bring so much love to Mariah. And Lord, I also thank You so much for the love that Mariah brings to our house with her smile and her laughter. In Your name I pray, Amen."

Mariah had brought a great deal of warmth and love to our home. Her infectious smile would light up the room when one of us entered. It didn't help any that she was a snuggler; she would snuggle deep into someone's shoulder when held, much like a koala from Kelly's homeland.

The visitations continued with the mother, but there was no father to be found. During the next few months, numerous potential fathers were named. Many of them were given DNA tests, and all failed. Others refused to have a test, or were unable to be located. Kelly and I often joked that Mariah wouldn't be able to date anybody in the five surrounding counties, as the person could be her brother or cousin.

Spring came upon us suddenly, as the perfume of flowers filled the air, along with the sounds of birds preparing for nesting season. I was preparing for a different season in my life, as well. After ten years at the high school in Eatonton, I turned in my resignation letter, with both excitement and sadness. I had made some dear friends there, and I genuinely enjoyed my students and the classroom. Yet, God's call to work in Monticello was strong and undeniable. With my classes for my master's in media technology ending in a month's time, I accepted a position as the media specialist at the high school in town, just three miles from our home. I was nervous, as I would be starting a position that was completely foreign to me, as well as work with people who I did not know; at the same time, I was excited for the opportunity to work in the town where my children were growing up and called home.

Summer was a whirlwind, and it seemed as if we were constantly on the go. Kolby and Jace both went to church choir camp that year, and all three of our children spent a week in Michigan with my parents. Gerard and Leisa spent some time with us before they returned back to Australia, their three year sojourn in the States coming to an end. We also continued our summer tradition of visiting the town square each Saturday morning for the farmer's market, as well as an ice cream cone from the local ice cream and plant parlor. I began work on another master's, this time in administration. To top it all off, we put in a salt water swimming pool, and our children soon immersed themselves in it for the rest of the summer. I considered calling in some scientists to examine the children, as I was convinced each of them grew a set of gills. Through all of this, Mariah bonded herself more securely to the family, and we became known in the community as the ones who were fostering the baby born at the hospital. Kelly even took her to the hospital on regular occasions to visit the nurses. She became one spoiled child, spoiled by hugs, kisses, and unending love. Before we knew it, summer had passed us by; as fast as the hummingbirds that fed at our many feeders, summer flew by like a colorful flash.

The new school year started, this time with both Jace and I entering into new schools. Jace joined Kolby at the Elementary school, while I was across town at the newly built high school, entering into a new career. My anxiety was quickly calmed, as I felt not only accepted by the unfamiliar staff, but welcomed, as well. I felt immediately at home, and enjoyed the new position and new challenge.

As Kelly and I firmly believed in raising our own children ourselves, instead of placing them into a day care environment, we had worked very hard to ensure that someone was at home with the children at all times before they went to school. Each of our three, before reaching school age, had attended a three hour three day a week Bible school at a local church, simply to give them some interaction with other children. Kelly would work in the evenings and weekends massaging, while I taught in the nearby county. When Brody entered kindergarten, Kelly began working during the days, ending when the children were ready to be picked up from school. Mariah, though, posed a new problem.

"Kelly, we didn't plan on having another child when you went back to work. Mariah is going to have to go to day care," I tried to explain to her.

"I know; I just don't like the idea of putting her into day care all day long. We didn't do it for our own children."

"No, we didn't," I reasoned, "but I don't believe that God will be upset with us if we place Mariah into it. She is already better off with us than she would be if she were with her mother. Besides, sadly, we don't have much of a choice. When we built this house, it was with the understanding that we both needed to work. That's why we waited until our own were old enough to attend school."

"You're right," she hesitated before going on. "It's just hard. She needs love, and she doesn't need to be there. I just feel guilty, that's all." I loved her for her guilt, and was happy that I married a woman who wanted to raise not only her own children, but others, as well, in her home.

The battle for Mariah began shortly before we were to leave for Disney World that year, and it left me drained. It also forced me to examine how much I had grown to love her as my own. It all began when Nancy called Kelly one day in October.

As she was still in jail, Mariah's mother had decided to give up custody of her ten month old daughter, instead allowing her twenty three year old friend to have custody. Kelly was devastated, her heart ravaged with an impending deep and profound loss. Our own children were also overcome with sadness and disconcertion. We had been asked the question by many of our church family if we would adopt Mariah, and Kelly had begun to seriously take it to heart. Kolby, Jace, and Brody already considered Mariah their sister, and were adamant, in their own way, that we adopt her. I, on the other hand, did not want to adopt her. Instead, I had been praying that our gift from God be adopted by a family who was not fortunate enough to have their own children. I felt selfish wishing to adopt her, when I had three of my own children, all healthy, all happy. God had blessed me abundantly, and I wanted a childless married couple to experience this same blessing. If Mariah could bring the same joy to a young couple as she had us, and if it was God's will, then so be it. I prayed for discernment daily in this, and was looking for God's will concerning little Mariah. I felt strongly, though, that His will did not have Mariah in this new home with the young twenty three year old, and I began to dig a little deeper into it.

"Nancy, I can't believe that this is the best place for Mariah," I passionately argued with the caseworker. She had just informed me that Mariah would be moving in with the twenty three year old who worked two jobs. The friend of Mariah's mother was also living with her forty six year old boyfriend. But what I found most alarming was who her boyfriend was. He was the father of two boys whom I had taught previously; both arrested at the school for possession of drugs. The more I learned about where Mariah was going to live, and who would be raising her, the more incensed I became. I was going to fight for her, a take no prisoners type of fight. After all, I determined, this was for Mariah's future, and she had no one else to fight for her.

"This friend of Mariah's mother," I continued, "is not the best person to raise Mariah. . Do you know if she smokes?"

"I smoke. You're just being judgmental, John," Nancy said.

"I'm not being judgmental; I am just looking after the health of this baby. When she was born, she had such a hard time weaning herself off of her mother's drugs, and we don't know what the long term effects are. Breathing in secondary smoke is certainly not going to be beneficial for her, or any baby for that matter." Maybe I was being judgmental. I probably was, as upset as I was over the situation. "I just can't imagine that this young girl can look after her properly. She holds two jobs, so when will she be able to raise Mariah, teach her, nurture her, love her? Is she going to allow her boyfriend to do it? The boyfriend who is twice her age, who's old enough to be her father….He can't even make a commitment to his girlfriend and marry her. How is he going to make a commitment to Mariah?" I stumbled over my own words, as I continued. "And I don't have much faith in his own parenting skills, as both of his own boys are in jail for selling drugs. I watched both of them get arrested in front of me." Yes, it was apparent to me, I was being judgmental, but I was beyond that. This was too personal to me. I didn't want to be in a position later on in life and bump into Mariah on the streets or worse, in need, in trouble, and regret not fighting for her with all I had in me; bruised feelings aside.

"I understand, John, but sometimes these things are out of our control," Nancy answered. "We can only give the judge the information, and he will make the final decision. Nothing is decided just yet."

"Well, if DFCS and the judge decide that the best place for Mariah is in this lady's home, than I am afraid that I can't do this anymore. I won't be a foster parent again, as we apparently have two different opinions on the welfare of this child, Nancy." Tense in the shoulders, I bid Nancy goodbye, and hung up the phone. I could feel a headache coming on from the tension.

Opening the drawer, I pulled out the phone book, and called up a friend of mine, an attorney, and explained the situation. Finishing, I placed another call, this time to another friend, a judge in town. Good thing for a small town, I thought. They both agreed to look into it, leaving me a little relieved, yet still full of concern. I did all I could, it was now in God's hands. So, how come I had a hard time giving it over to Him?

CHAPTER 7

Lindsey's mother Amy stayed at our house while we were at Disney World. Our old babysitter's mother had fallen in love with Mariah, and considered her a third daughter. Mariah was simply too young to take to Disney World with us, and Amy volunteered to undergo the battery of paperwork, police background checks, and everything else that went into the investigation which the state conducts when caring for a foster child. Kelly and I attempted to leave our worries about Mariah's future at home while on vacation, and tried to make it a great trip. Both of us, though, were uneasy through our entire stay, as Mariah was scheduled to leave our home the weekend after we came back, and not even Donald Duck could fully cheer me from that.

As I arrived home from work the Wednesday after Thanksgiving, I walked up the stairs to find Kelly in full grin mode. She looked like the Cheshire cat, beaming with delight. "Guess what?"

"Ah...your three time great aunt had a hangnail back in 1897." I enjoyed this game of guessing.

"No, I..." Kelly was obviously excited about something.

"I get three guesses. You discovered that you really do enjoy Pat Boone in a black leather jacket." This was fun.

"No. Stop guessing," she smiled. "Mariah is not going this weekend."

"What?" My heart leapt out of my chest, and was sitting squarely in the center of my throat.

"Well, Nancy called me up today and was talking about Christmas presents for Mariah, and I asked, 'Isn't she going this weekend?' and Nancy said 'Oh, no, that's not happening anymore.'"

"Wow!" This was great news; news which I found very surprising. Confused, I asked, "So....what does that mean? Will Mariah be going to her grandmother, or will she be going to another home?"

Kelly's smile disappeared somewhat, as sadness entered her eyes. "I don't know, Nancy didn't know, either."

"Hmm....ah well, this is great news, anyways. Guess we just need to keep on praying."

"Yes, pray without ceasing, 1 Thessalonians," Kelly said. I was grateful for my wife reminding me of the truth of this verse, as I bent to kiss her. We didn't know what the future held for Mariah, but I felt a little more reassured as I remembered that God was in control.

Shortly before Christmas vacation, I was visited by Mary, a DFCS caseworker from a nearby county. She was touring the high school with some foster parents from our county, Lisa and Bill, along with their new foster child, Helena, a seventeen year old. Wearing a soft smile on her face, Helena's eyes told another story. She looked timid, frightened, and alone, as if she were completely helpless and lost. Once more, my heart reached out to her, and I tried to be as kind and warm as I could. I had not met a foster child that old, and I felt particularly sympathetic for her. As Mary thanked me and continued along the way with Helena and Terry to register her into school, Lisa stayed behind to ask me a couple of questions. After answering them, I reassured her that I would look out for Helena, and help to ease her transition as best I could.

Once again, Christmas was upon us, and this year, Mariah joined in on many of our celebrations and events, including the church Christmas caroling, making her the youngest one that year. Neither Kelly nor I had the opportunity to carry her that evening, as she was passed around from loving arms to loving arms the entire time. It was only after dinner was over and we were heading back to the car that we once again held her. I marveled, as I often did, about how blessed Kelly and I were to have such a loving and supporting church family. We would not be able to foster without them.

Lynne and Steve once more were Mariah's foster grandparents, helping us out with her presents, and Amy joined in to spoil her even more. My parents joined us over the Christmas vacation, and our house was again saturated with joy and laughter.

It was a Thursday when we got "the call," again. Kelly was planning on going away with some of her friends for the Martin Luther King Jr. weekend. This time, "the call" took place in my office at work, as Mary came to visit me at the high school. I had only met Mary one time beforehand, when she visited the school with Lisa and Bill and their foster child, Helena, so we spent a moment or two to get to know each other a little better. Then, Mary hit me with it, leaving me stunned.

"Mr. DeGarmo, we need another home for Helena. Would you and your wife be willing to take her in?" Her smile faded a bit, as the seriousness of the question sank into me. I almost fell off the chair, in a most undignified manner, as my mind went blank. We already had Mariah, why on Earth would DFCS ask us to take in another child, a teenager no less?

"Ah….um…..uh…" I fumbled the question; failed in my response. I was floundering around like a seal out of water. My eyes darted from one thing to another, trying to focus in on the correct response. Heck, any response would be better than what I was doing. Recovering, I said, "Mary, I have to talk to Kelly about this first. I am not brave enough, or courageous enough to answer that question by myself. I don't have proper authority to answer for her." I was grasping at trying to poke a little humor into the topic, as I felt the heaviness of the possibility of fostering another child beginning to block my breathing. I picked up the phone and called Kelly at work. Fortunately, she was between massages, and I quickly explained the situation to her.

"Boomie, I have to go give another massage, so I don't have much time. Just find out all the information you can, and then make a decision. Make sure you pray before you do anything."

I said a silent prayer to myself as I hung up the phone. Turning to Mary, I asked "Okay, what can you tell me about her?"

"Well, this is Helena's third adoption, and her family placed her into custody of DFCS shortly before Christmas, when you first met her."

I interrupted, raising my voice a little. "Third adoption? Did you say that this is her THIRD?"

"Yes, that's right," Mary continued. "Helena is originally from Romania. When she was nine, her parents died, and she was placed in an orphanage with her older sister and two brothers. Helena was adopted by a family in New York, and lived with them for a year, where she was abused, and then returned to the state. A family from Pennsylvania then adopted her, and after six months, they returned her, as well. We don't have any information on these two adoptions, and Helena remembers very little. After that, a family here in Georgia adopted her. That was six years ago. They also adopted her sister. She has a brother somewhere in the U.S., and another one still in Romania, though we can't trace either one of them."

I was stunned, yet again. How in the world could a family adopt a child, and then after six years, give the child back to the state, to foster care? And this had happened three times to this young teenage girl. It would explain the look of fear and loneliness I saw on her face the month before, when she first entered into the media center. "This is awful," I said to Mary. "How in the world can a child function after being adopted three times and then returned back to foster care?"

"I know," is all Mary could reply.

"So, why in the world did her parents give her back?" I was more than a little upset by this. How cruel, I thought to myself.

"Well, I don't have all of that information just yet. We believe that there were drugs in the house, and maybe some abuse. Her mother just dropped her off at DFCS one morning on the way to school, and said that they were finished with her. She was a wreck, John, and that's when she went to Bill and Lisa's house. But they can no longer take her."

"Mary, I have to tell you that Kelly and I have a policy where we are not going to take foster children into our house that are older than our children, as we don't want our own kids exposed to things they aren't ready for just yet."

Mary nodded her head. "I understand."

I took a deep breath, and then released it in a drawn out sigh, trying to gather my courage. "But.....we'll take her in. She needs somebody, the poor girl. I feel so bad for her!"

"Can we call her into your office and explain it to her?" Mary asked.

What? Now? My brain was screaming out to me. I NEED A MINUTE! Instead, I looked at Mary, saying, "Sure, I'll just find out what class she's in, and call her over the intercom." Wow! And Kelly was going to be away this weekend. Was I ready to do this by myself, all five kids, for the weekend? I quickly floated a prayer up to God, asking for strength, as I asked for Helena to come to the media center.

As she entered, I smiled and offered her a chair, allowing Mary to do all the talking. Helena wore the same smile she had on when I first met her, one of loneliness, as Mary explained to her that she would be going to another family. As I sat there, listening, Helena asked Mary about the family.

"Well, Helena," Mary smiled, "that's why I called you in here. Mr. DeGarmo and his wife would like to take you in. How does that sound?"

"Oh!" the Romanian born girl answered, in surprise. "I wondered why I was in here."

It was my turn. Lord, please give me the right words to say to this child, I silently prayed to myself before speaking aloud to her. "Helena," I said, "we have another foster child at our house named Mariah with us, plus I have three children of my own. We would be very happy to have you come and live with us."

"Okay....." she said, meekly.

"Now, I need to tell you that we do have rules in our house, but I don't think you will have any problem with them." I quickly realized it wasn't the best thing to say. I had to rebound, get this back on track. "My wife's from another country, like you, and I think you might really like her."

"That's right, Helena, Mr. John's wife is from Australia," Mary helped out. Helena simply sat there, not knowing what to say, not trusting. After all, I was simply another adult to her, another one who would most probably betray her, abuse her, and throw her out into the street. How could she trust me? How could she trust anybody? This was going to take some time.

Mary brought Helena to our house after school the next day. I met the two of them at the car, Kolby holding Mariah, with Jace and Brody trailing behind me. Kelly had already left with her friends for the weekend. Grabbing Helena's suitcases, I invited both of them inside and showed them Helena's room, which used to be our guest room. Mary informed me that DFCS had bought a dresser and mirror for Helena, and that it would be delivered in a few days, while I volunteered to paint the room any color the teenager wished. Once again, her quiet smile spread across her face, as she asked for pink.

That first weekend sped by quickly, as Helena and my own children helped to watch over Mariah, while I painted her room. Throughout the day Saturday, and into Sunday morning, Helena was filled with dozens of questions about Kelly, seeming eager to meet her. When Sunday afternoon rolled around, a few of the teenagers from our church came by and took Helena to church youth group with them, giving me some time with my own children.

"She's nice, Daddy," said my ten year old, Kolby, "and she's really pretty."

"She has really nice hair," Jace chimed in. Helena's Romanian heritage clearly showed, as her dark complexion and raven colored hair bespoke of her place of birth. I had asked her questions about her time in Romania, with her claiming very little memory of it. Perhaps she had placed a wall in front of that memory, to block part of the pain of the experience, I thought. I was not psychologist, though; that was Kelly's strength.

Perhaps I should have read the signs early on. There were certainly plenty of them. Maybe I was just being too optimistic, or maybe I was just plain blind. As they say in the South, "I reckon I wuz blind."

It was midway through Helena's first week at school. I was eating lunch in my office when Helena walked in, tears flowing down her face, and her voice cracking. "Mr. John, I hate it here. The other kids are so mean to me."

"Here, have a seat, sweetheart. I know its hard being at a new school," I said, trying to comfort her. "Tell me what's wrong."

"The other kids in Monticello are just mean. There's a girl in my automotive class that's just picking on me, and saying things that's not true." Her shoulder shook, as she tried to control her sobbing. I continued to listen as she spilled forth her story.

As she finished, I put my arm on her shoulder. "Helena, I'm glad you came and told me about this. Miss Kelly and I are going to be here for you when you have problems. We aren't going anywhere. Please know this; my office is here for you when you need it. Now, let's get a drink of water for you before you go back to class, and I think you'll feel better if you splash some cold water on your face."

"Yes sir," she said, quietly, as she followed me to the kitchen area. Leading her back to class later, I felt relieved, happy that this crisis was over, and pleased that she came to me with it. That night, after Mariah and our own children had gone to bed, Helena sat by the fire with Kelly, telling her about the experience, and very animated. She seemed to delight in Kelly's attention, as she laughed and smiled. I noticed throughout the next few weeks how much she enjoyed being around Kelly, and would try to carve out time with her each night. Helena also came to enjoy caring for Mariah, as well. Perhaps it was because the teenager recognized the fact that they were both foster children, living in a stranger's house. Or, perhaps it was the magic spell that Mariah seemed to weave upon all who met her. Probably a little of both, I felt.

Mariah had begun crawling, and Kolby, Jace, and Brody were beside themselves with enthusiasm. Heck, they were bouncing off the walls in excitement, as they tried to coax her to take her first steps. We had fallen into a routine each day, as best we could. Kelly and I would get up ahead of the children to have some prayer time, with me putting in some early minutes for daily exercises, as well. Then, we got the children up, fed, dressed, and out the door. Kelly would take the younger kids to their school before heading off to a full day at work, while I took Helena to school with me, as she began her day with her 11th grade classes. Many evenings each week saw Kelly working while I fed and bathed the little ones, as well as helping with homework if needed. Tuesday nights saw me driving an hour away for my class for my educational administration degree, and the nights were late ones, as I would often get home long after the children were in bed for the night. Kelly continued her doctoral classes online, applying what she learned into our lives. She soon had us eating better; so much better, in fact, that the two of us spent a week fasting in an attempt to cleanse our colons. It made for a very long week. It was a busy time; it was a tiring time.

The second Father Daughter Dance was held on that second Friday of February, drawing an even bigger crowd this year. I had worked hard to make it a more enjoyable night than the previous year, and was again looking forward to it. This year, I had the honor of escorting four young ladies; my two girls, Mariah, and Helena. I had asked her to come with us, and she seemed excited to attend. Since it was short notice for her, we borrowed a prom dress from a church member, and all four girls looked great. All the girls at the dance that night were beautiful. It was like Cinderella's Ball. The two hour dance was electric, as the excitement filled the church's fellowship hall. Dads kicked off their shoes and danced the Hokey Pokey with their daughters, taught them the words to "Shout," and the gestures to "YMCA." I was sweating half way through the night. At one point, though, Helena burst into tears, and ran towards the ladies bathroom. I stood the helpless bystander, as my heart reached out to her.

"Daddy, should I go see what's wrong?" Kolby wanted to know.

"No, honey, not just yet. Let's give her a minute, and then you can." I wanted to give Helena the privacy she needed before we intruded. After a few moments, Kolby went into the bathroom to see if Helena needed any help.

"She said she's lonely, Daddy, and missed her home," Kolby let me know as she returned. I suspected that was it. After a few minutes, she rejoined us, and I tried to give her a reassuring smile. Reassuring! How could I reassure her? What would I reassure her about? The dance continued, and all had a great time, though Helena's loneliness did damper it a bit for me the rest of the night.

The next sign that all wasn't as well as I would have liked came soon. I missed that sign, too. Helena had become friends with some students that Kelly and I found were we not so fond of. It had been two months since she came to live with us, and we had been encouraging her to make new friends and to keep her grades up. Helena's school work continued to be excellent, and I marveled at it. How could this girl, who's been through so much, through the death of both of her parents and through three adoptions, how could she focus so clearly on her school work? Most children would simply give up from all the pain, suffering, and rejection. Helena was determined to graduate from high school, and I began to plant the seed of going on to college afterward.

It was her choice of friends, though, that had Kelly and I worried, with us both thinking it would lead her to trouble. Sure enough, it did. Helena had befriended a student who was repeatedly in trouble at school, and who was habitually absent, as well. As we didn't want to chase Helena away from us by putting too many demands upon her, we simply stood by and were observers, praying for her along the way. While I saw her throughout the day at school, I was able to keep an eye on her without interfering. One night, Helena approached Kelly and I about having her friend stay the night. I had been filling in Kelly with my concerns about the friend, though I looked for her lead on this decision.

"It might be good for her," my wife said. "Helena needs friends. I know it's going to be crazy, but let's try it."

I was a little concerned when the girl's father did not call our house to verify if his daughter could come over. More than that, I was disturbed that he didn't call to make sure that his daughter wasn't going to the home of an "ax murderer, or worse," as Kelly put it. So, as the girls sat on our porch that Friday afternoon, I called the father up, reassuring him that all was fine, and asked him when he would like to pick his daughter up. After some mumbling, he told me he would the following afternoon. Giving him directions, I hung up, thinking all was well.

Saturday came, and no call from Dad. Both Helena and her friend seemed to be having a good time, laughing and giggling like teen aged girls do. Saturday night rolled around, and still dad did not call, so we invited Helena's friend to stay with us again. Certainly he would call Sunday morning. After taking her to church with us the next morning, I finally told Kelly that I would simply have to take her home, myself, that afternoon. She didn't seem the least bit fazed, showing no signs of worry or concern. When I reached her father's home, I was alarmed by the state it was in. Filth and garbage strewn from one end of the yard to another; a wheel-less car rusting away; house looking like it might fall in on itself. It was very gloomy; very scary. I said a silent prayer to myself, asking God to help protect this young girl, and to deliver her from such a frightening looking environment.

The real trouble, though, started the next day, Monday, when Helena came into my office midway through the morning, complaining that she was sick. Leaving a message on Kelly's answering machine to let her know, I took Helena home, and returned to work. It was noon when Kelly rang me back. She had immediately suspected something was wrong, that something was troublesome when she heard my message.

"Boom, something's not right," earnestness ringing through her Australian accent. "Remember when I told you I heard a noise in the night Saturday night, sounding like a door opening and closing?"

"Yes, I remember." I had told her when she woke me that night that it was her imagination. Where was this leading to?

"I think maybe she was up to something. I'm going to call her right now. I'll call you back later. Love ya."

"I love you, too. Thanks Kel." I was hoping that she was way off on this, but I had a bad feeling that her instincts were probably correct.

A half hour later, I knew she was right. "Boom, do you know why she went home today?" I could hear the anger in my wife's voice. Feeling my shoulders begin to tighten up, I replied I did not. Boy, this wasn't going to be good.

"I told Helena I knew something was wrong and that she better tell me EVERYTHING right NOW!"

The tightness in my shoulders was spreading into my neck. "What did she say?"

"Well, that was her and her friend, Saturday night, sneaking out at around midnight. They went and met some friends of theirs at the stop sign up the street, hung around them for a while, and snuck back in the house."

"Oh no....," I moaned. My jaw was now rock solid, tense as ever. "What are we going to do?"

"We're going to go home after work and have a long talk with her. Boomie, we can't have her doing this. It's teaching our kids the wrong thing. Besides, this is just too stressful. I'm having a hard time relaxing in the house." Helena's mood swings were difficult on both of us.

"I agree hon. It's hard for me, too." Five kids in the house were beginning to drain me, and I wasn't ready for the teenaged drama yet. "Let's pray about it throughout the rest of the day, and you and I will talk to her when we get home." We said our goodbyes, and finished the day at our jobs. When I arrived home later that day, Kelly was waiting for me in the kitchen, handing a Sippy cup to Mariah. After kissing her and saying hi to the kids, we both headed downstairs to face Helena. I was apprehensive, not sure where the conversation was going to take us. Kelly, though, was very sure, and took control. We knocked on the door.

"I don't feel so good." Great! Helena was in one of her negative moods, I could tell immediately, by the tone in her voice.

"Open up this door right now, young lady!" Wow! I don't think I ever heard Kelly speak this way to anyone before. This was something new, even for me, and I was a tad bit jumpy, myself. We entered the room, and Kelly let Helena know in no uncertain terms that she was not too delighted with the seventeen year old, nor was she overjoyed with Helena's behavior, either. "Helena!" she continued, focused on making a strong impression, "we care far too much for you to allow you to sneak around. What if you got hurt? What if someone else hurt you?"

Seeing Helena's confused look on her face, Kelly softened, but remained firm. "Helena, this is a different house, and we are going to have different rules than your previous home. We love you. We would be crushed if anything happened to you. Our rules are meant to keep you safe, and only have your best intentions in mind. You might not see that right now, but these are the same rules we will have for our own children when they reach your age."

"Helena, Miss Kelly's right," I continued, "we do love you. You are part of our family, and we are going to do our best to protect you and to help you. You will be punished for this, and we are disappointed. But, that doesn't mean we will stop loving you. Okay?"

"Yes sir," she answered. She didn't believe us, and I didn't blame her in the least. She had been hurt too many times to trust in two strangers, like Kelly and I. But, we did love her, and hopefully this seed of love had been planted deep enough that it would start to grow, and maybe even blossom.

Sensing that all were tired, Kelly and I said goodnight. As I closed the door, I took a long look at my wife, as she leaned against the wall. "Boomie, I don't know if we can do this…" she wondered aloud, her eyes filled with confusion and weariness. I made no comment. I didn't know myself.

Chapter 8

For some time now, I had been praying for God to find the right family for Mariah to live with, a family that needed her, and a family that God would bless. But it was becoming more and more apparent to me that God had other plans for Mariah. The signals were all there, I just wasn't opening my heart to them.

"John, I sure hope you adopt her," Amy would continue to tell me each time I saw her.

"How are your kids going to handle Mariah going to another home?" Lynne asked me at church one Sunday.

"I couldn't do what you do," said Cathy at church choir practice. "It would break my heart having to give her back."

Kelly seemed to be the ringleader. "Boomie, I'm going to be devastated if we don't adopt her. It will be like taking one of my own children away from me."

It would break my heart, too. Though I did wish for her to be adopted by a loving family, I knew that it would be devastating to me to give her up. What I feared, though, was that the baby I had been raising for the past fifteen months, since she had been born, would go to a home where she would not have what she needed in life to succeed. I feared about a home where she might be mistreated, a home full of drugs, a home where she would suffer. I realized that I had to fight for her once again, this time, for keeps.

As the beginning of April approached, we received a letter from DFCS that Mariah's mother would be having a custody hearing at our local courthouse, and that we were welcome to attend if we wished to.

Mariah had been in DFCS' custody for over a year, now, and the time had come for the state to determine if Mariah would remain in the custody of her mother, or be placed with another family member. If no family member came forward to take custody, she would be placed up for adoption. As we were the foster parents, we had first rights to adoption. Perhaps everyone else was right. Perhaps we were meant to adopt Mariah.

I awoke the morning of the trial a nervous wreck. Neither Kelly nor I had slept all night, and Kelly had decided not to attend the court case. "I just can't, Boom. I can't take the stress. You go for us," she told me the night before. As I put on my suit and tie, I said an extra prayer. Kelly took Brody, Jace, and Kolby to school, while I remained behind with Mariah, as the case wouldn't be heard until nine that morning. Sitting down at the dining table one last time to read my statement, I rocked Mariah in my arms, holding back the tears that were rising up to overwhelm me.

It was a beautiful day outside. Daffodils were abloom in our yard, and the mock orange was flowering, its well known aroma perfuming the air. The snowball bushes and the Yoshino cherry trees were also in full force, blossoms covering one of end of those trees to another. I took a deep breath, inhaling the smell of spring, and buckled Mariah into her car seat, hands trembling as I did so.

Parking outside the local ice cream parlor, I scooped her in my arms as I walked into the court house. The historic building had been featured a few years back in the film My Cousin Vinnie, as it was a product of another era, of the Old Deep South. We climbed the steps, walked through the large superior court room, and entered into the magistrate's waiting room.

"Hi John," Nancy said, as she walked up to meet me.

"Hi. How are you?" I wasn't really in the mood for this, but I put on the smiling face as best I could.

"I'm good. Listen, Mariah's mom wants some time with her before the court case." Not what I expected to hear. And I certainly didn't want to hand over Mariah to her right now. This was hard. It dawned on me that this might be it, that Mariah might be leaving us. Today!

Right now! Sweat started dripping down the back of my shirt, and my knees began to buckle, just a bit. This WAS hard. Glancing around, I saw her mother out of the corner of my eye. She was sitting in one of the chairs outside the court room, alongside her own mother and a police officer. I noticed straight away the handcuffs and prison outfit adorning her. I tried to throw a smile her way, but had no luck, as she was boring a hole in the carpet in front of her with her eyes.

"Uh...okay..." I said. That's all I could say, no other words were coming to me. I felt as if my own child were being taken from me. Anger flared up inside me, as I followed Nancy into the waiting room. The police officer and Mariah's mother soon followed behind us. Unlocking the handcuffs, the officer exited the room, as the mother and Nancy sat down.

"Do you mind if I hold her?"

"Sure," I forced out, with a strained grin. I placed Mariah into her arms, and stood back, waiting. No way was I leaving the room now. Deep inside, I knew I was being selfish, perhaps even rude. But, this was a fight, and I wasn't going to surrender easily. Mariah began to cry, squirming like babies often do when they are uncomfortable. Her mother tried to comfort her, with no luck, and soon handed her back to me.

"John, I just want you to know that I've changed and that when I get out of prison, I'm gonna to be a better mother. I also want to thank you and Kelly for all y'all've done. If I can't have her," she said, her face wet with tears, "my mom's gonna get custody." My jaw quickly clenched.

"Well..." I began, taking a deep sigh and releasing it. "I have to be honest and tell you that I don't think that's the best plan for Mariah. I feel that...." Another sigh, lips pursed together. I had to do this. I had to get this said. "....that....we can provide for Mariah in a different way." I was treading carefully, trying not to upset her, but it wasn't working. I had to be bold, and not worry about feelings. "We're going to fight for her."

"Excuse me, folks, but court's about to start," the bailiff told us, poking his head in the door. Handing Mariah over to Nancy, I headed over to the court room, and took my seat in the middle of the room. Unlike the superior court room, this smaller juvenile court room was modern, with plush benches, and a flat screen TV alongside the window. Nancy entered next, with Mariah in her arms, followed by the attorney who was representing the case. Mariah's grandmother was already in the room. Last in were Mariah's mother, and her jailer. Spread throughout the rest of the room were about two dozen or so others; some waiting for their own case, some supporting Mariah's mother, or some simply there to pass the time of day. Shortly after all sat down, the bailiff re-entered, asking all to stand, as the judge completed the menagerie of participants. His black robe nearly matched his grayish hair, and black rimmed glasses. He smiled at all in the room, as he indicated that we could sit back down. A friendly face, I thought, one who might be on my side. At least, I was praying that this was the case.

The judge ran through the cases to be heard that day, four in total. I wasn't sure if the fact that ours was first was a good sign or not. It was by no means hot in the court room, but my shirt and palms were already wet with sweat.

"The court calls Jones vs. the state of Georgia. Are all in attendance?" The judge looked over his glasses, into the audience.

"Miss Jones is here, your honor," the DFCS representative said. After the judge looked over the various paperwork that were lying in front of him in order to further familiarize himself with the case, he then proceeded to ask the DFCS attorney to begin her opening statements.

I sat nervously in the middle of the room as the attorney commenced to recount the mother's recent history, her continuing rehabilitation from her drug addiction, and her progress in jail. I grew more anxious when the attorney then explained, in great sweeping detail, about how the mother had made improvements in her development as a parental figure. Furthermore, the attorney declared, the mother had made concrete plans to find employment after her release, and had already secured a place to live, for both her and her two daughters; Mariah and her older half sister.

Throughout this testimony, my heart raced, threatening to leap out of my suit coat, as I began to feel Mariah slipping away from our family. The attorney was excellent in her delivery, and I would have readily employed her as my own personal lawyer if I ever needed one. Was she too good?

The judge next asked if the foster parents were in the courtroom. As the caseworker said that I was to the judge, I also indicated my presence by raising my hand. Looking towards me, he then asked Nancy about Mariah's care under our roof. The DFCS caseworker quickly gave a summary about Mariah's life within our household, and informing the judge that she was well looked after and living in a stable, secure, and healthy environment. I waited for the judge to make his ruling, waited with the obligatory baited breath. Ironically, I had recently taught Shakespeare's Merchant of Venice, where the phrase originated. Now, I was using the great writer's phrase as my own, as I fretfully awaited the judge's decision.

Looking up from the papers on his desk, the judge cleared his throat, which brought all eyes back to him. The anxiety in the room was heavy and oppressive, and I could feel the apprehension loom in the room for both myself and Mariah's birth family.

"The placement of a child is an important decision, a decision that I do not take lightly," he said, taking off his glasses to further study the courtroom. "A child such as Mariah needs a home where she is loved, and where she has family. It is apparent that Miss Jones has taken great steps in her rehabilitation, and I commend her for that," he said, pausing to look at Mariah's birth mother. "It is difficult, and I acknowledge that," he continued, "and I believe that you have come a long way. You still have a long way to go."

"I know, Your Honor," she replied. She, too, was nervous, as her face was flushed with the possibility of losing her daughter.

My daughter, I thought to myself.

It was up to the judge to determine whose daughter the baby girl was.

"Miss Jones, you have had over a year, now, to fulfill your obligations with DFCS, and as I have said, you have made progress. Yet, you have failed to complete these obligations. Mariah needs to be a in a home, now, with a family. Therefore, it is the court's ruling that Mariah become a ward of the state."

As in many courtrooms, there were two very different emotional releases upon hearing the judge's declaration. Mariah's mother burst forth in anguish, her sobs plain for all to hear in the small chamber. Placing her arm around her daughter's shoulders, Mariah's grandmother tried to console her own young daughter.

On the other hand, I felt a great weight lifted from my heart, hearing the pronouncement. Mariah was ours. Tears began to form in the corners of my eyes, as the joy of the moment welled within me. But the joy was only to last for that moment, as the judge began to speak again, raising his voice ever slightly, to accommodate for the peals of sadness ringing from the opposite side of where I sat.

"Does the Department of Family and Children' Services have another home in mind in regards to custody of Mariah?"

"We do, your honor," Nancy said, as she stood up to face the juvenile courtroom judge. "Miss Jone's grandmother has agreed to take custody of the child."

The momentary elation I felt suddenly crashed, as the joy drained out of me, quickly replaced with a feeling of dread. Oh, no, I thought, this can't be happening. Please, Lord, please deliver her to us; please allow Mariah to stay with us. My prayer was a pleading one, as the urgency of the moment pressed down upon me. As my prayers hurled towards Heaven, Mariah's biological grandmother took the stand next to the judge and was sworn in.

During her testimony, the older Miss Jones, when asked if she had a steady source of income, noted that she had been working for a while at the same job. The judge then questioned her about where she was living, as he tried to discern if the living environment for young Mariah was suitable and stable or not.

"I live with my ex husband, sir," she said.

"And how long have you been living with him?"

She fumbled with her answer, as she struggled to come up with the proper response, a response that the judge would find feasible.

"Um…a while now." My heart, which was leaping out of my chest moments earlier in elation, was now beating violently against my chest in distress.

After a few more questions, the judge then asked the casa worker if she would like to offer her opinion on the matter. Casa workers are those individuals who act as advocates for the foster child, and are strictly volunteers. Fortunately for us, Mariah's casa worker, Joan, was deeply interested in our baby Mariah's well being, and had not only visited with us often, she had apparently done some investigating on her own, uncovering some information that was vital to the future of this precious child, as we were all about to find out.

"Your honor, I have spoken with Mr. Marx, and he told me that he doesn't want Miss Jones to move back in with him."

"Oh?" the judge looked upon Joan with curiosity.

"Yes, sir. Mr. Marx said he's tired and he wants to live alone. He said he doesn't want to take care of any more children, either."

"Mrs. Jones, what do you have to say to this?" he asked, turning to the grandmother.

"Well, sir, I am going to move there. Me and him, we've worked things out for my daughter to move in with us, and little Mariah can come and live with us, too. It's all okay," she said.

"I have a letter here from Mr. Marx," the elderly caseworker continued, indicating towards the biological grandmother, the one seeking to take Mariah out of our lives, "and he says that she is not living with him, and that she is not going to live with him, either.

"May I see the letter, please," the judge asked. A moment or two elapsed as he read it, after which he turned to the elder Miss Jones. "Miss Jones, this letter is apparently from your ex husband. In it, he clearly states that you will not be moving in. How do you respond to this?"

I straightened up, stiff in alertness; perhaps there was hope after all. My eyes were riveted upon the grandmother as I listened to her response. "Well…I'm not sure….I don't know…" was all she could say, faltering in a response.

After further discussion with the judge, Mrs. Jones stepped down from the stand, and took her seat next to her daughter. There was clearly a different atmosphere, a different mood, in the room, as if a different pathway were now being set upon. "Would the foster parent like to address the court?" The words of the judge snapped me to attention. I had prepared for such as this by writing out a statement. Still, my heart beat rapidly, even more than before.

"Thank you, your honor, I would," I said, as I stood. Taking the folded paper out of the inside pocket of my suit, I enfolded it, and took a deep breath. Strange; I had sung in front of thousands, performed on Good Morning America, and been in front of large audiences during wrestling events, as well. Yet, my nerves were never as wrought as they were that moment.

"Mariah has not only become a part of our family, she has become our child to my wife and I. As with any of our children, we have hopes and dreams for her, and have begun to plan for her future. My wife and I are able to provide for Mariah not only a stable home, but a loving family, a safe environment, and the possibility of a bright future. I believe that we are better able to provide her many more opportunities and many more resources than she would be provided in the home of Mrs. Jones. My wife and I have stable incomes, secure jobs. Education for all of our children is important to us, as well as their health, and I feel we can provide both. It is my fear that Mariah will not be able to thrive, not be able to prosper in the environment that Mrs. Jones would provide. I also have grave concerns that Mariah would not have a home to live in if she were in the custody of Mrs. Jones. I ask the court to deeply consider placing Mariah into our care, permanently, and I ask for permission to adopt her. Mariah has known no other family except our family, has known no other mother than my wife. She has developed no relationship with Miss Jones, or with Mrs. Jones. There is no mother daughter relationship between them, a relationship that is vital to her emotional stability. Furthermore, there is no father daughter relationship between her other than between her and myself, simply because the birth father has not been identified, despite numerous attempts. Your honor, I feel that placing Mariah into any other home would not only harm her emotionally, but would be detrimental to her future and her well being. Thank you."

A mixture of feelings washed over me. I was relieved that I had the opportunity to address the judge, to fight for my child. At the same time, I felt a little guilty; I had not wanted to be harsh in regards to Mariah's mother and grandmother. Yet, if I had been overly concerned with their feelings, Mariah may have been very much lost to us. I did what had to be done, though I wasn't proud of it.

After a few more rounds of questioning to both the caseworker and the casa worker, the judge placed his pen down from writing. Straightening the papers upon the large oak desk he sat behind, the robed judge looked at the court room, passing his eyes over all in attendance, with a smile.

"Ladies and gentleman," he began. "I wish to thank all who came and testified in behalf of this little child. Thank you, Joan, for all the work you have done as a casa worker. Your contributions have been important, and I appreciate the fact that you have volunteered many hours on behalf of Mariah. I also want to thank those of you who work at DFCS; your job is often very difficult and may even seem unrewarding at times. Your service to these children is vital, though, and so very important.

"It is easy to see that Mariah is very loved by her mother, her grandmother, and her foster parents. She is very fortunate in this regards. Yet, she will need more than the love of a family in her life in order to be successful. It is apparent that her foster parents are able to provide a more secure and stable home for her. Along with this, Mariah has known no other family besides her foster family. It would be harmful for her to move her to yet another home. Therefore, the court approves the adoption of Mariah Jones to her foster parents. Thank you, and congratulations, Mr. DeGarmo."

As the judge smiled at me, I grasped to take in fully what he had said. Oblivious to those around me who were also smiling in my direction, I began to cry. Was it true? Was it over? My mind grappled as I tried to wrap my brain around the thought; Mariah was ours. Mariah was ours! I shook with elation, and wiped back the tears. Kelly! She had to know! First things, first, though. I had people to thank, the judge,

Nancy, the attorney, Joan; I was beyond grateful to all of them, and shared my appreciation with them before leaving the courtroom.

Waiting outside in the lobby, Nancy smiled and handed Mariah to me. I smothered her with kisses, as I enveloped her in my arms. Seated next to Nancy was Mariah's birth mother, still in chains, alongside her own mother. Awkwardly, I smiled at both of them.

"John, promise me I'll be a part of Mariah's life," my officially new daughter's birth mother pleaded, her face awash in tears.

"Yes, of course," I reassured her, quickly wanting to get away. I was uncomfortable with this. Plus, I really wanted to tell Kelly the news.

"Thank you," she got out, between sobs. "Please remind Mariah that I love her."

"Okay, I will," I replied, holding Mariah in my arms.

Moments later, I dropped Mariah off at her "school," a local church which had as its ministry a "Mother's Morning Out," a service which provided a place where small children could be looked after for a few hours in the mornings, allowing mothers to have a break from their motherly responsibilities. Giving my daughter another round of kisses, I dashed off to Kelly's work, where I found her between massages.

"Well....?" the Australian said, with great hesitation. She feared the worst. Instead of giving her a quick reply, I lost it. I lost it completely. A flood of tears came crashing forth, as I let my emotions flow freely and unabated. The tears coming so strongly, I was unable to give voice to the wonderful news to Kelly, leaving her believing that we had failed. "Tell me!" she demanded, in concern.

".....she's ours.....she's ours...." I managed, before falling into her arms.

CHAPTER 9

It was as if a heavy load had been lifted off the shoulders of Kelly and I. Mariah was ours, a part of the family; she was going to be a DeGarmo. All we needed to do was sign the adoption papers, and our family was going to officially grow by one. I could breathe much easier, and I was most grateful to God for this gift. Kelly and I started to make concrete plans for her as our newest family member.

"What do you think about Grace?" Kelly asked me, shortly after the court hearing. We had been working on giving her a new name. "As in, God's grace; God's free gift of love."

"Yeah, it sounds good to me. What do you want to call her middle name?" When it came to Kolby, Jace, and Brody, we had some long, long, long debates about their names. With Mariah, I didn't feel like going down that road again, instead just pretty much going with what Kelly had in mind.

"I think we should keep Mariah as her middle name, as its part of who she is."

"Hmm…..Grace Mariah DeGarmo…has a good ring to it. Okay, that works for me. Good choice, Mrs. DeGarmo. Now, I've got a question for you. I want you to seriously consider something. It's been on my heart for awhile, now."

Kelly stopped for a moment with the dinner preparations, and looked at me. "What's that?"

"Well, I've been thinking about the adoption thing. I feel really bad for Helena; she has no real family of her own, no family to call her own. I would like to offer her the option to adopt her." Kelly wasn't expecting this, as her eyes grew larger, and jaw dropped a shade. I pressed on, "I want to offer her a place to call home when she's older. Kelly," I became more impassioned, arms gesturing, "When she's in college, where is she going to go when she has Christmas vacation, or any vacation? When she's married, where is she going to take her kids when she wants to take them to their grandparents for Christmas? Since we are adopting Grace, this might be a great time to offer to adopt her, as well. I want to offer her our last name, so she can have a family in her future."

Kelly took a moment, collecting her thoughts. This was sudden, not at all what she expected. After all, it had been difficult with Helena. She had resisted fully embracing our family rules, morals, and lifestyle. "I don't know, Boomie. I don't think she WANTS us to adopt her. She probably doesn't…"

"But, she might," I said, shrugging my shoulders. "We don't know. We can at least offer her, give her the opportunity. Can you pray about it?"

"It's a big move, Boom. Yes, I'll pray about it, and think it over. She…." We were interrupted by Helena coming into the kitchen. She was smiling, and in a good mood. Her mood swings, which she suffered sadly from, often left us wondering what manner of spirit she might be in, from one moment to the next.

"What are y'all doin?" she asked.

"Oh, just having a talk, hon," Kelly said. Our discussion would have to continue another time. Frankly, with five children in the house, it was difficult to get more than two minutes alone with each other to have an "adult conversation." Instead, those discussions were usually relegated to the night time, when we both settled into bed for the evening. The bedroom; it is the secret conversational domain for all parents.

The next day, the same conversation came up again, in the same location, with almost the same results. Almost, but with one major change; the end result. It was after school, and I had cornered Kelly in the kitchen again, trying to see her frame of mind on my earlier proposal the night prior. "I still don't know, Boomie. I'm nervous about it. I guess we could ask her and see what she has to say…"

"Hey, y'all. What'cha doin'?" Helena asked, as she topped the stairs from the basement. Her Romanian dark looks were accented by her bright smile.

"Well, Helena…." Kelly said. As if to throw me a cue, she looked directly at me, waiting for me to pick up the dialogue thread she started.

"Helena," I began, returning her smile. I was nervous, too, but excited at the same time. Were we really going to expand our family by two children in the space of a few days; without the whole birth process? I never was much of a fan of that, after all; too nerve wracking. This wasn't much easier, though. "Kelly and I have been praying about this, and we would like to offer you our last name. You have become a big part of our family, and we love you very much. If you would like, we would be happy to adopt you, at the same time we adopt Gracie." Leaning against the kitchen counter, I waited for Helena's reaction. She stood in the center of the kitchen, with a polite smile upon her face. Without much hesitation, she replied "Okay."

"Are you sure, honey? We don't want to force this upon you," Kelly said, placing a hand upon her shoulder. Kelly's warmth and loving heart were open for both Helena and I to see, easing the tension of the moment in the room.

"I'm sure," pausing, and then "it's fine," the seventeen year old said.

"GREAT!" I said, embracing her in a hug, and kissing her on the forehead. Kelly then followed my hug, with a deeper one of her own. It was set; our family was now going to grow to a total of seven. We were treading Brady Bunch levels, here.

Since becoming a parent, I had become a lot more conservative in my opinions and approach. When I was a teenager, I was always on the lookout for shock value, always seeking opportunities to embarrass those around me. I enjoyed a hearty laugh, and took immense gratification in bringing that laughter to others, as well. As for dating girls...well, I was a sheer Romantic, with a capital R. Flowers, candy, serenading, poetry; I pulled out all the stops when trying to impress any pretty face I saw.

But when it came time for someone to date my own daughters, I wasn't so eager. Any Romeo that came looking to win the hand of my girls was going to have a rough go of it, and jump through the many hoops, snares, and various examinations I was more than prepared to set up. So when Helena asked Kelly and I if she could go out on a date with a boy from town, my stomach started lurching. IT"S NOT MY TIME! I wasn't ready for this. I was supposed to have a few more years before I entered the dating world of my daughters. In fact, Kolby was not allowed to date until she was twenty seven, and then it had to be in a double date, with Kelly and I.

"Relax, Boomie, this is a good thing," Kelly told me. "I think we should allow her to go, as long as we make clear to her our rules and expectations." Calm down? How? And more importantly, WHY? Why should I calm down? I needed some advice. It was Sunday, and the date was this coming Friday. Sitting on the front porch swing outside, overlooking the newly planted daylily bed, I called up a host of advisors, those church members who had older daughters, who had braved these uncharted waters of mine, and who, I felt, steered through these murky waves with ease. First up was Steve, who had two daughters in college. Next up was David, who had a daughter in high school. Finally, I asked Adam, whose own daughter was a year older than Kolby. Even Ken gave me some advice, though he had no daughters of his own. Perhaps in a strange, and conceivably disturbing amalgamation, I combined all of their ideas into one grand scheme of my own, mentally and emotionally preparing myself for what would be a practice round before my own girls ran the dating obstacle course.

"You mean you need to meet him first? Why?" Helena stood, asking me, and, looking positively disgusted with this old fashioned fossil standing in front of her. Her date was minutes away from coming over.

"Because, honey, I love you, and it's just the right thing to do….." I was stammering. I wasn't ready for this. IT WASN'T MY TIME YET! Nonetheless, I pulled myself together and gave her the best reasoning

I could. Sighing, and giving me that look, that one look like I had no clue in the world, she went into her room and finished getting ready. Five minutes later, HE arrived. Zach. The wonder dude. Let the games begin.

"Hi, I'm Mr. DeGarmo. I'm Helena's foster father," I said, walking out to meet him. Extending out my hand to shake his, my face was set in a scowl. My dramatic skills were coming into practice here, as I began playing the part of a disgruntled and protective father.

"Hi, sir, I'm Zach," he said, shaking my hand in return. Polite, good eye contact, well mannered so far. But so was Eddie Haskell. I was on my guard.

"Come with me, son." Turning on my heels, I headed down the driveway and towards the back garden, without waiting for him. Entering into the garden shed, my next command sprang forth. "Here, put these on, and come help me, please, while we have a little talk," I said, handing him a pair of gloves. Pointing to two hay bales, I asked him, "please pick up one of these, and let's go spread some straw," while I picked up the other. Minutes later, the two of us were placing the straw on some new cucumber and tomato beds. I threw an array of questions at him, such as what his plans were after high school and his five and ten year goals. I felt a little like Steve Martin in the film "Father of the Bride." Now, it was time to bring in the heavy artillery.

"Zach, Helena is like a daughter to me. I consider her a part of my family, and I am going to watch over her like any father would."

"Yes sir."

Taking a page out of my friend's Steve book, I then added, "Her curfew is eleven o'clock. If she is even one minute late, I will assume that you have kidnapped her, and you are planning on not returning. At eleven oh one, I shall call the police, reporting it. Do you understand?"

Looking a little nervous, he replied, "Um….yes sir."

Now, it was a page out of my friend's Ken's book. "Good. Now my friend Ken tells me that I should add this, so I shall. Whatever you do to Helena, I am going to do the same to you. Now then, shall I kiss you now, or when you return?"

His face turned pale. His eyes were darting back and forth, looking for an avenue of retreat, but there was none. I had taken command, like a general in battle. He paused for what seemed like the length of an entire Michigan State football halftime, before stammering, "Uh…. um….when I …get…back?"

"Fine, I shall be waiting for you. Thanks for your help in the garden, I appreciate it. Let's go see what Helena is doing." I made it. I had maneuvered through the mine field that came when one's daughter was in the dating realm. Now, I was ready for my own girls' future dates.

It was ten fifteen when Helena walked through the door. I was watching a Bela Lugosi film, while Kelly was upstairs working on her doctoral studies. "That was the most boring date I've ever been on before," she sighed heavily, before walking upstairs to relay it to Kelly. Victory was mine!

It seemed that five children in our house weren't enough by DFCS' standards, or even God's. We received "the call" again, this time in mid March. Helena was on a date with Zach, and Lindsey was home from college, babysitting our children. Kelly and I were on our first date together in well over a year, and had just sat down for dinner at Applebee's when her cell phone rang. Noticing who was calling, she grew slightly nervous, a worried smile crossing her face as she looked up at me. "It's Mary," she said, referring to Helena's caseworker. Was something wrong with Helena? Had something gone awry on her date? I looked over the menu as she answered it and spoke with the DFCS employee. A deep sigh escaped from her as she finished the conversation, her face pale with anxiousness.

"Well, is anything wrong with Helena," I wondered.

"No….it's not that…Boomie, there's a four year old boy, and Mary wants to know if we want to take him?"

I was incredulous. It took a few seconds before I could find my voice. When I did, I replied "You've got to be kidding! This is a joke, right? Our first night out, and we haven't even ordered dinner yet?"

My heart dropped into my lap, as I sat there, staring dumbfounded at Kelly.

"Mary's waiting for me to call her back. I told her that I would talk it over with you, and we would make a decision."

My turn to sigh came, and I let one that echoed Kelly's just a moment before. I was tired. Five kids in the house, I didn't want to have six. I couldn't do it. "Well, what did she tell you about the boy?"

"Not much. Mary just said that he's four, and that he has a sister and a brother that are going to another home, closer to their mother. That family can't take three kids. Boomie, what do we do? I'm exhausted. I don't think we can....?"

"We need to pray about this," I said, as I reached across the table, taking her hands in mine. "Lord," I began, "we thank You for this opportunity to go out together. We also thank You for Lindsey at home with our children. Lord, we are tired, and don't know what to do. If You would have us take this boy in, please give us a sign; open our hearts to Your will. Amen." As I let go of Kelly's hands and opened my eyes, I looked to her for a reaction. "Well, what do you think?"

"I think we're crazy!" she answered.

"Yeah, we are." I paused. "So, are we going to do it?"

"I think so, what do you think?"

"I think so, too. It's what we do. We foster," I said, beginning to laugh, part from the situation, part from exhaustion. Kelly called Mary back, and we headed for the exit.

Scotty came that evening, a four year old boy whose smile instantly won everyone over he met. Mary gave us the details as we signed the paperwork. Scotty's father had beaten his older brother. Along with this, Scotty had been a victim of malnutrition, as all of his teeth had rotted out. Scotty's vocabulary was extremely limited, as he could speak no more than two words at a time. His older brother and younger sister were with a family three hours away, closer to their mother, while his father was in jail. Mary did not know how long the little four years old would be with us. "No problem," I said, "just keep us posted, please."

The next few weeks were dizzying ones, as we adjusted to six children in the house. We became a two car family, as we could no longer fit all eight of us in the van. Going to church became a challenge each Sunday, as we now had to get another small child ready. Fortunately, Helena stepped up to the plate, and hit a home run. She was wonderful with Scotty, helping him with breakfast and taking care of him. She fell for him, as she had Grace, and took him under her wing. We could not have done it without her.

Scotty was an eating machine, his stomach a bottomless pit. It mattered not to him that he did not have teeth, he swallowed anything in sight. His battle cry became "Me Hungry." Very quickly, he made an impact at church, as well, as our church family once again embraced a foster child of ours. Each time we reached church, we were met with many hands and loving arms, reaching out to scoop various children up from our tired limbs.

I felt God's hand in our church one Sunday in particular. It was the first Sunday in April, and the men of the church had gathered together at a local baseball field to play the boys in a game of softball, followed by a cookout. Scotty's skills as a baseball player were completely nonexistent. Obviously, this toothless eating machine had never picked up a baseball bat, nor thrown a ball in his life. But, when he came up to bat each time….well, what I witnessed was a small miracle. Scotty hit a home run not only the first time, but all four times he came up to bat.

Without any word or suggestion from me, the men had determined that Scotty, who had experienced so much pain in his short life, was going to have a day to remember. As I helped Scotty hit the ball, the entire outfield became suddenly clumsy. Not one of them could pick the ball up to throw it. Scotty rounded the bases each time to a chorus of cheers, as each of my church family members rooted him on. Scotty's toothless grin shined as bright as the sun that day as the members of my church reminded me of why I fostered, a reminder I needed, a reminder from God.

It had been awhile since Kelly had gone to Australia, and she missed her homeland desperately. The pull of her native country, her family, and all that she was familiar with was strong, and it was time to make another visit. Besides the tremendous distance between the two, another challenge to a cross cultural marriage was the cost. Tickets to the Land Down Under were not cheap, and this time, all of our own children were no longer "children" in the eyes of the plane industry; it was full price for both Kelly and I, and three children. That fact didn't tickle my fancy!

Yet, that wasn't the only obstacle that we faced. What were we going to do with the three children that we were not taking; Helena, Scotty, and Gracie? We couldn't take all of them with us, DFCS would not allow it, nor would our wallets. Lindsey's mother, Amy, helped us out; first, by agreeing to house sit for us, and second by taking care of her angel, Grace. Scotty would go and stay with another foster family a half hour away. Helena, though, was different. We had been working for some time to get a passport for her, as Mary agreed with the two of us; a trip to Australia might be just the thing she needed. Kelly's large extended family was by far the most loving family I had encountered, and I was certain that they would treat her as family, embracing her as one of their own. Our only holdup was her birth certificate and proof of United States residency. These papers were held by her adopted family in the nearby town, and they were refusing to hand them over to Mary. Despite pleas by the DFCS caseworker, they would not budge. Without them, Helena was unable to get a passport, and sadly was unable to accompany us to Australia. She would have to stay behind with another foster parent, here in Monticello.

Kelly and the two girls left a week before Spring Break, and I was alone with the other four children. My evenings were full, as I prepared meals for the four of them, did washing, and helped Brody with his school work. Helena helped out with Scotty and Grace in the mornings, and lifted some of the workload from my shoulders. Friday came, and it was time for Brody and I to leave, ourselves. I dropped Scotty off at his day care with his suitcase, Grace went to hers, and Helena came to school with me with her suitcase, as well. All three of the children would be picked up by their respective caretakers. After school, I picked up Brody from school, and we headed to the airport. It was a fierce storm that we battled on the way to Atlanta, a thunderstorm the likes I had not seen for some time, lighting up the night sky with flashes and shaking the car with its thunderous booms. After a four hour wait at the airport, the airline notified the weary would be travelers with the discouraging news that the flight was cancelled. The storm was too much. Dejectedly, Brody and I headed home, placed a call to Kelly, and hit the pillows, the storm still ringing in our ears. The next day, we were on the plane, and soon in Australia.

The time flew by quickly. We called and spoke with Helena a few times, as well as baby Grace, and both were fine. I also placed a call to one of our neighbors, Libby, who was looking after the animals; pigs, goats, turkeys, ducks, cats, and a pony. We had established a small petting zoo over the past two years, in hopes of bringing some animal therapy to the foster children, something I had read about.

"John, I'm afraid I have some bad news for you," Libby said. I could hear the discomfort in her voice, even through the poor phone connection.

"What's up?" I asked.

"The pony....well.....I'm afraid Precious is dead. She died the night you left, during the storm."

Not what I wanted to hear! Not Precious! "Oh my goodness, Libby! I'm sorry you had to go through that." Darn it! I really liked that pony. When one of Kelly's client's passed away, his wife gave us the pony, along with some goats. It wasn't the friendliest one, but it was a pony! The romantic in me dreamed of my children galloping through fields of amber on it, wind blowing their hair as they clung to her flowing mane; never mind that Precious was over twenty years old and only had one eye.

"I found it dead, leaning against a tree. I think it was struck by lightning during the storm," she went on. I thanked Libby for all she was doing, and apologized once again that she had to experience something that was not on her agenda. After hanging up the phone, I told Kelly about Precious, expecting her to feel the anguish I felt, to experience the dismay that I was undergoing. Instead, she laughed. She laughed and did not stop laughing. She became hysterical. Apparently, this was funny, and I reacted the wrong way.

"What's wrong with you, Kelly? Precious died. She's dead. This is bad news." Obviously, I needed to help Kelly through the shock she must be feeling.

"The kids never enjoyed feeding her, Boomie. They didn't like her, she was always biting them." To prove her point, Kelly called each of the kids in to deliver them the alarming news. Their reactions only underscored that I was the only one upset. I was met with smiles.

"Daddy, she always bit me," Jace exclaimed.

"I didn't like feeding her every day," my son offered.

"Yeah, Daddy, and I didn't like having to brush her. She was mean," my oldest daughter added. Poor Precious; I was the only one grieving for her. No fields of amber, no flowing manes. My dreams were ended.

Scotty underwent his own painful experience while we were away. As his teeth were all rotted out, he was in sore need of some choppers, something to help him in his never ending quest for food. "Me Hungry" was heard throughout our house hourly. Teeth, any teeth, would aid him in this hobby of his. After a few visits to the dentist and a surgery, Scotty was fitted with a set of artificial teeth. When we picked him up after returning home from Australia, he beamed with pride the rest of the evening, showcasing his new teeth. I was happy for him, yet upset at the same time. Again, I felt the sting of anger towards his parents, letting his teeth get to the point where they would rot out. Children at age four need not undergo the pain of surgery due to the neglect of those who are given the honor of raising them. Scotty was a gift to his parents, as all children are, yet he was not treated as one. How could parents hurt their children like this?

Ever since Helena entered into foster care with Bill and Lisa, she had been seeing a psychiatrist each week. I was amazed at how stable she was after all of the major trauma and upheaval she had encountered in such a short time, and I knew that if I were in her position, I would need a lot more than a psychiatrist to help me through. Mary had asked us if we would meet with him after we had announced to her that we were planning on adopting the teenager, and we happily agreed to. It was a pleasant meeting, and we learned a lot more about her, which aided us in helping her. The big meeting, though, took place two weeks afterwards, when Helena met with her adopted mother of six years, the father refusing to come. It was necessary, in order for our adoption process to continue, for her mother and father to give up their rights to her. They refused, with no explanation. I was confused; why would a family adopt a child, abuse her, then voluntarily give her back to the state by dropping her off on the way to school one morning at their county's DFCS, and yet be unwilling to give up their rights to her? It was an ugly meeting. The father sent word through the mother that as far as he was concerned, Helena was no longer part of his family and that he wished her good luck. The mother was even uglier, throwing many hurtful and destructive comments Helena's way. What was even more disappointing was the fact that the couple refused to give us any of the paperwork they had in regards to Helena's birth certificate and legal entry into the United States. She left the meeting a tearful wreck, even more confused than beforehand. Our only way forward lay in DFCS going to court to legally take the rights away from her previous family.

It was Wednesday in mid April when the next sign came that all was not as it seemed. The plans after school called for us traveling to a nearby city, meet up with Mary, and begin the necessary paperwork in order to get the adoption process onto the next step. Mary had organized for Helena's family to have their rights taken away, and we were to sign papers for the adoption agency in order to proceed. The school bell had rung, and the hall had filled up with students, rushing to catch their buses or to the student parking lot and drive home. I waited for Helena outside the library, eager to get going myself. This was a big day for us, and I was anxious to meet up with Kelly and Mary. The usual flow of students heading home was different, though. There was a large commotion on the other end of the hallway, and I sensed that something was amiss. As I headed down to see if all was well, a student ran up to me, breathless, and with a look of concern strapped across her face.

"Mr. DeGarmo, Helena's been in a fight! She's down there," pointing towards the assistant principal's office. Without hesitation, I headed quickly towards the office, my mind ablaze with apprehension. What in the WORLD was going ON? This can't be right? It must be another student.

Entering into the assistant principal's office, I found her sitting down in a chair, looking ashen. Briefly explaining the situation, the assistant principal left me alone to confront Helena. Instead of praying for wisdom and guidance, as I should, I lost my cool. All those months of stress and tension from Grace's court trial, master's classes, Kelly's doctoral work, Helena's own mood swings and adoption challenges, plus my own three children, I snapped. "What are you doing?" I demanded, raising my voice, with a mask of anger. I was in no mood for silly excuses, as I understood the severity of the situation at hand. We were to be at the adoption meeting in one hour, yet Helena was facing a trip to the local sheriff's department. As she was over sixteen, the school's policy on fighting stated that students could be handcuffed and escorted to the county jail. She froze, saying nothing. I had never displayed this level of anger or frustration with her before, and she was uncertain what I might do. As the sheriff entered into the office with the principal's assistant, I picked up the phone, leaving messages with both Mary and Kelly about the situation. This day was quickly becoming everything I didn't want, a complete disaster.

The school's assistant principal explained to Helena the consequences of her actions, while she continued to sit there, silent. I had not seen this side of her, as a look of hopelessness colored her face. The sheriff then placed the handcuffs upon her wrists, leading her to the patrol car. I followed behind her, myself speechless, though mine was from the sheer frustration I was feeling. I felt a sense of betrayal from her.

Hours later, after she has spent roughly four hours in jail, Ken accompanied me as I picked her up and brought her home. I needed the adult support that night. Tension does not begin to describe the air in the house for the rest of the evening. Kelly and I laid down the law with her, while at the same time telling her we weren't giving up on her. "Helena, I'm very angry and very disappointed with you. You are never going to do that again, while you live with us, do you understand young lady?"

"Yes, ma'am."

"And don't think you are going to leave us. You're stuck with us, whether you like it or not. Do you know what "unconditional love means? It means that no matter what you do or say, we are still going to love you, regardless. No conditions. We love you, and are always going to love you, no matter what." At this, Helena looked down, wordless at this new term in her life. After I echoed Kelly's sentiments, we said our goodnights, and headed upstairs to try and figure out what to do next.

It wasn't until Helena met with her psychiatrist the following week when we discovered what really was happening, and it brought me to tears. Helena had only experienced pain, rejection, sadness, and disillusionment with three other adoptions. Her past had taught her that adoption led only to unhappiness and heartache. Why would an adoption by the DeGarmo family be any different? So, in an attempt to sabotage it, she willingly caused the fight the week before by seeking out another student immediately after the bell rang, and attacking her. In no way did I condone her actions, but I understood them. Hers was a life of constant betrayal by any and all who said they loved her. In her mind, even her parents betrayed her by their death when she was but a small child, resulting in her and her siblings being split up and placed in homes with strangers in a foreign country. At nine, she was parentless, living with strangers, and forced to learn English, a language that was not her own. Helena was simply trying to survive as best she knew how.

For the remainder of the school year, our relationship with Helena was different. No longer would she come and talk openly with Kelly; she no longer laughed as much with the children, and her affections towards Grace had dimmed, as well. There was sullenness about her, as well as sorrow. We continued to pray for her, and reaffirm our love, but were met with a wall that she had placed before her. Something had to alter as the strain was wearing on all of us. Sadly, something did happen, which left me with immense guilt and grief.

The friction in the house became overwhelming to the point that Kelly and I sat down with Helena during the first week of summer vacation. We had been in great prayer about it for weeks, now, and decided that a change had to be made to bring an end to the suffering that all were feeling in the home. As Kelly has a better sense of what to say in the affairs of all things children, I let her do much of the talking. Helena remained silent as we explained to her that she had to live with our rules, our morals, and our values, instead of simply living in our home to use the TV, the refrigerator, and the pool, as she was wont to do of late.

"Are y'all kicking me out?" It was the only question she put forth that night.

"No, honey, we're not. We're not making that decision, you are. You have to choose which one you want. You can choose to live with our rules and our values, or you can choose to live at the youth group home that Miss Mary, your caseworker, spoke about. We love you, and don't want you to move, but the choice is up to you."

Three days later, Helena began arguing vehemently with me, defiant in both words and action. Sadly, I walked away, and placed a call to Mary, informing her that Helena had made the choice to leave. It wasn't a call I wanted to make. An hour and a half later, our house was one person emptier.

The weight of my guilt lay heavy upon me for some time. I kept replaying the events in my head, trying to discover what I could have done differently to thwart Helena's moving. Did we not love her enough? Did we not offer her more flexibility in our home? I grappled with this daily, though Kelly continued to reaffirm to me that we had done all we could with Helena. She wasn't willing to meet us half way at that point in her life, as she had had too many betrayals of her own. She couldn't fully trust us, as she was waiting for us to hurt her, like all those parental figures that had come before us. Kelly's words rang true to me, yet I could not escape my personal guilt. I let her down. She needed someone in her life to help her, and I let her down.

Except for a brief phone call the day she left, we did not hear from her for some time. I began to write her letters every two weeks, and left messages on her machine. After two months had passed, she returned a call. My heart soared! Packing the kids in the car, Kelly and I drove the hour trip to see her, taking her out to dinner. I once again sat across from my Kelly, amazed at how my wife found just the right words to say to a hurting child. Reaffirming our love to Helena, Kelly expressed to her that she was still part of our family, she just couldn't live with us right now, but she was welcome to come and visit any weekend and any time she wished. We also reassured her that we would always be there to help her in any way.

Driving home that night, I felt the remorse that lay upon my heart lighten a little. Helena was in a place that could look after her, perhaps better than we could. Even so, our family had grown to love Helena deeply, and her absence from our household left me remorseful. It tore me up. It still does.

CHAPTER 10

The power of prayer is an awesome thing. The fact that God listens to our prayers and answers each and every one of them in His way and His time is not only comforting, it is reassuring. Though there have been many times when I couldn't see or hear God's answer, after some time had passed, I could always see His hand in our lives, and in our requests to Him. What is even more reassuring is that with God's blessings, anything can be accomplished. Matthew 19:26 tells us "With God, all things are possible." I have come to rely on that verse, and embrace it, as both Kelly and I tackle each challenge that lie ahead of us. I learned to lean upon Him even more so, as our house grew larger, and our lives even busier as each month passed. Without God, I wouldn't be able to do it, wouldn't be able to foster.

To be sure, I was not always fond of being a foster parent. It is a difficult job, one that exhausts me both physically and emotionally. I have at times become very angry with birth parents for the abuse and neglect they place upon their children, and coming to feel that some adults don't deserve to have children. Visitation days were days where Kelly and I had to pick up the pieces of a child's broken dreams of going back home, thus often destroying much of what we had earlier accomplished with a child. The system also frustrated me, all of the rules and regulations that DFCS expected and placed upon us, as foster parents, were often difficult to work with, and left one frustrated. Yes, there was, at times, very little joy in being a foster parent.

Yet, I clearly heard God's call to continue fostering in my life. The need was so strong, and there were so few willing to do it, to pick up

Jesus' cross. Christ tells me to "Pick up My cross and follow me," in Luke 9:23. He doesn't say, "And have a great time doing it, you'll love it, it's really easy." As much as I would like to, I can't ignore this call in my life, this mission. I remind myself that we are here to serve Christ in all that we do. I am comforted with God's word when He tells us that we shall receive our rewards in Heaven.

When you have a number of children come through your house, like we have, you begin to discover things about yourself. I found that Kelly and I could do anything we put our minds to. It wasn't really that hard. Whether it was Kelly working on her doctoral, my two master's courses, serving as an Elder in our church and fostering five children, including Grace, as well as the three of our own, Kelly and I just did it. Even so, we were tired, depleted, and lacked energy. I often heard the same question put forth to me "How do you do it?" My response was always the same, "Lack of sleep, lots of prayer, and God's grace."

Once again, though, we found ourselves with only five children in the house for a period of time, and it felt good. The house was a little more peaceful and quiet, at least as quiet as it can get with five children, including a year and a half old toddler, in Grace. Helena left us the first week of that 2008 summer vacation. Though my guilt lay heavy upon me, I did allow the stress to slowly dwindle from my neck and shoulders, as I fully embraced the summer and all the promises it held for my family and I. I love summer, I embrace it, and I savor each moment of it, and was ready to take full advantage of it. Gardening, late nights, swimming, reading, watching Bela Lugosi films, time with the children, time with my wife; ah, the promises seemed endless in what was certainly not an endless summer.

Kolby journeyed to New York City for a week with my parents, enjoying the sights and sounds of the Biggest Apple there is. Upon her return, the three older kids spent a week at the Vacation Bible School a number of our churches co-hosted. Another week saw the same children attend the church choir camp in the northern part of the state. In between those adventures, Kolby, Jace, and Brody grew back their gills from the previous summer. After breakfast each morning, they hit the pool running, spending a few hours swimming and laughing, swimming and playing. Mid afternoon, they were back at it, emptying the pool of water as they splashed back and forth, jumping in and out, and doing their best impression of an Olympic swimmer. Finally, shortly before bedtime, they would close the day out with another pool side visit. Kelly would often join us in those evening swims. All the while, Grace would test the waters, learning to swim in her own way. Why we never had a pool before was beyond me.

My second masters had come to an end, and with Kelly's encouragement, I began my own doctoral studies. Watching Helena and Sydney struggle with their emotional and behavioral challenges while in school led me to focus my doctoral work in that area. As a foster parent, I had seen the emotional turmoil that foster children face on a daily basis as they struggle with feelings of rejection, frustration, sadness, confusion, and a host of other emotions stemming from their situation. As a result, school is often last on their priorities. Helena still amazed me in her personal quest to succeed in school, despite all of these challenges.

As a high school teacher, I had also been witness to my foster children encounter other teachers who had no skills or resources available to them to best aid these children, many of the children thrust into a new school, new county, and new environment. I had struggled, myself, in trying to best help the foster children living with me, and have had to watch, sometimes helpless, as schools, caseworkers, and child welfare agencies fail in their attempts at best aiding these lost children. Thus, I decided to devote my doctoral study to not only the foster children in my own home, but to foster children everywhere, as I attempted to find solutions to this tragic and heart wrenching situation. The real challenge, though, lie in trying to find time for both Kelly and I to work on our school work, along with all the other responsibilities we had. We just charged ahead, and did it, ignoring those around us who told us we were crazy. We knew, and we were okay with it. After all, one has to be a little crazy to foster.

It was mid June when I received a phone call that shook me and troubled me at the same time. Kelly and I were in the kitchen, preparing dinner, while the four older children were playing on the swing set.

Grace was coloring at the table. It was a peaceful summer night. Kelly was home from work, and the plan of attack was to eat dinner out by the pool, cheering on Scotty as he continued his swimming lessons from me. The peace, though, was about to be shattered; shattered by a phone call that would leave us all questioning.

"Hello," I answered, as I cut up some carrots.

"Is that you, Daddy?" a familiar voice called back to me.

I was speechless for a few seconds, as my mind raced to figure out who it was on the other end of the line. "SYDNEY?" My jaw must have hit the table, as I was stunned, dropping the knife onto the floor in the process. Twirling around from the stove, Kelly immediately stopped what she was doing, herself startled by my surprising answer over the phone.

"Hi, Daddy, it's me." It was Sydney, all right. She sounded timid, though, not the Sydney I remembered, not the ball of laughter and loud voice that lived in my house for a year and a half.

"Sydney, where are you!"

"I'm in a foster home in Alabama," she said. I recalled quickly that the last time I had spoken with her was the day she left us to live with her aunt and uncle in Florida. What had gone wrong? Why was she in another foster home? There were too many questions flying through my mind, and I knew that Kelly could handle this conversation better than I could.

"Just a minute, Sydney, let me get Miss Kelly. I know she would love to say hi." I handed the phone over to my wife, as I stood next to her, hoping to pick up bits and pieces of the conversation.

"Hi, sweetheart! How are you?" Kelly asked with excitement in her voice from talking to one who we thought was lost to us.

"I'm in a foster home in Alabama, Mommy. I want to come home, and live with y'all." Kelly's smile dropped, her heart plunging to her feet, as a pale of sadness entered into the conversation.

"Well, honey, I....I..." Unsure of how to respond to Sydney's startling exclamation, Kelly then asked, "Sydney, I thought you were in Florida with your aunt and uncle."

"Yes, ma'am, I was. But they tried ta strangle me, so I was put in another foster home, here in Alabama. They're real nice, but I want ta come back home."

"Sydney, is your foster mother there right now?" Remembering Sydney's remarkable storytelling fabrications, Kelly thought it best to get the foster parent's side of this disturbing news.

"Yes, ma'am. I'll git her for ya. Jest a second." Kelly glanced over at me, with a look of sorrow registering on her face. "Boomie, she wants to come home, and live with us!" she whispered urgently to me. I had no words, still not over the initial surprise of hearing Sydney's voice on the line after these few years.

Kelly put up a hand, indicating to me that someone was talking to her, and that I needed to remain silent. I sure wasn't about to say anything right now, as I wanted to hear, myself. "Hello, I'm Susan, Sydney's foster mother. How are you?"

"I'm fine, thanks. I'm Kelly. I used to be Sydney's foster mother. She came to live with us four years ago. She stayed with us for about a year and a half before she went to live with an aunt and uncle in Florida, right before Christmas. How long has she been with you?"

"Oh, she just came to us about a week ago. She was in Florida, with her aunt and uncle, but was removed by DFCS. I'm not really sure why, just that there was some physical abuse. When she came to us, she only had two things in her possession; a pink pillow with a picture in it, and another picture, with your name and phone number on the back. Someone had written something on the back that brought tears to my eyes, when I read it. I asked Sydney who was on the picture, and she said her family. She wanted to call you. I hope you don't mind."

"Oh! Not at all! We've been wondering how she was doing. Maybe Sydney could come and spend the summer with us. We are off to Michigan for next week, but maybe after that, she could come and stay for awhile." I nodded to Kelly in agreement. This was happening rather fast, and I was glad that my wife was leading the conversation.

"Well, that sounds nice," Susan agreed. "Let me talk it over with the caseworker while you are away. Do you have any information you can give me about Sydney?" Kelly spent the rest of the phone call filling in Susan about Sydney's time with us. When she was finished, I had a million questions for her, as I normally do, but Kelly had no answers for me. Sydney had just moved in with Susan and her family, and they had very little information about Sydney to begin with.

Four days afterwards, Kolby, Jace, and Brody flew up to Michigan and spent a week up there, while Kelly stayed home and worked, and I looked after Grace and Scotty. The next weekend, I drove up to Michigan, myself, spending a few days with my parents before driving the long sixteen hour drive back home with the children in tow. I was on my way home with them, when I received a call from Kelly. She sounded tired, but quite calm. It was Saturday morning, and she was at home with Grace and Scott when DFCS called. Two small children were found by the police wandering down a country interstate highway, and needed a home for the day, immediately. A four year old girl and her one and a half year old brother had walked away from their home. Apparently, DFCS told Kelly, the two lived with their grandmother, who was often away from home while she worked, and she often left the children by themselves. One Saturday morning, the two of them decided to go for a little walk outside the house, ending up on the interstate.

I listened, as Kelly told me that DFCS was looking for a permanent placement for them, calling up various foster families for help. Yet, the children needed a place while they called, as it was considered an emergency, and Kelly agreed to take them in. I was flabbergasted; how could she look after four very small children by herself? I reaffirmed my love for her, prayed for her over the phone, and hung up. Quickly calling up Steve and Lynne, our volunteer foster grandparents, and explaining the situation to them, I asked if they could go to our house and act as reinforcements, helping out while I was away. I was worried for Kelly, and I believe my concern was evident in my shaking voice. When Lynne graciously agreed to head there right away, much of my concern faded away, and once again I was thankful for our church family.

It was quite late when I made it home that Saturday, and Scotty and Grace were already asleep. So, too, were Kolby, Jace, and Brody, in the car, and I carried them inside, with Kelly helping me to get them to bed. I was eager, though; I wanted to hear of Kelly's adventures with the two other children, before hitting the pillow for some much needed snoring time.

"Well, Steven and Lynne came over to help, Boomie. Did you call them up?" she asked, with me nodding in return. "Thanks. It was an answer to a prayer," she continued. "The two children were found by the county sheriff and placed in DFCS' custody, and they called me for help. They were so filthy, Boom, kinda like Sarah and Mary Lou were; just covered in dirt over their entire body. The four year old girl couldn't talk at all. All she did was grunt. It was so sad," Kelly's voice softened, as she spoke, with the sadness of the girl heavy on her mind. "I bathed them, and fed them, while Lynne and Steve looked after Grace and Scotty. They were such a big help! I couldn't have done it without them."

"That's great. I'm glad I called them, I was so worried for you, honey, and felt powerless, not being here to help."

"The little girl, Boomie; you should have seen her. She couldn't speak at all, just grunted in a sad way. I wrote down her name, and then helped her write her own name. It took awhile, but when she did, she just started clapping, and got so excited. It was really like a Helen Keller moment. Lynne and Steve stayed with me until another caseworker came and picked up the two in the evening."

Clearly, Kelly was even more exhausted than I was from her long day. We both spent a moment, however, with bowed heads, thanking God for my safe return home with the three older children, as well as the safety and wellbeing of the two children who He brought to our home that day. Though a very short fostering experience, only lasting the course of a day, it appeared that it was a positive experience for Kelly, and reminded us, once again, why we do it; why we foster. The need was too strong not to, and God had dropped into our lives two of His precious children who needed help, allowing us to share His love with them, and giving us love back in return.

During this two week time, Kelly and Susan, Sydney's foster mother, had been playing phone tag, each missing the other, and leaving messages on answering machines. When they had finally caught up with each other, three weeks had passed since that surprising night when Sydney first called. What Susan had to tell Kelly that night was disturbing, and even frightening.

Sydney's foster mother informed Kelly that Sydney had run away from their home, taking with her their five year old son. Though he eventually made his way home, after a frantic search by the foster parents, Sydney did not return on her own accord, hoping to make her way to Georgia. Was it to see us? Perhaps. That surely is a likelihood. As Sydney was nowhere to be found, the Alabama Bureau of Investigation was called in, and she was eventually located.

"Sydney has been through a lot; much has happened to her since she lived with you, and none of it is good," Susan told Kelly. "What she knows now is scary, and you might not want your own children introduced to what she knows." Kelly listened, as Susan told the Australian of some of the discussions Sydney had had with her new foster parents. "We can't have her in our house, after what she did to our son, and have had to turn her back over to the state. She's now in a home for girls, as she is deemed 'unadoptable', due to her age." The last term, "unadoptable," hit Kelly like a sledgehammer. With tears welling in her eyes, she thanked Susan for the call, and sank into the nearby chair.

"Dear Lord," she prayed, "please look after Sydney. Please protect her from any more harm or danger that she might face. Lord, we love Sydney, and ask that You help us contact her. She's only a little girl, Lord, only eleven. She shouldn't have to suffer anymore. And Jesus, thank you that my own children are safe. Please protect them. Lord, I don't want any hard lessons with my own children. Amen."

After much prayer, Kelly and I decided that we would like Sydney to come and visit, if only for a week or two in the summer. Yet, we found that the Department of Family and Children Services in each state do not communicate with each other. Georgia's DFCS had no record of where she might be, and were not able to help us in locating her. But, Sydney was a part of our family; she had lived in our home for a year and a half. She had traveled to Disney World with us. She had laughed and played with our children. She was dear to our hearts. We were not about to give up on her.

Summer continued to fly by, much too quickly for my likes. Time getting my hands dirty in the flower beds was all too fleeting. When time did allow, I was elbow deep in the soil, planting and pruning. Silence often reigns in the garden, and I found solace in it. A garden is often a place where I can often collect my thoughts, and quietly ponder on the challenges that were facing my family. It was one such day when Kelly rang the dinner bell by the house to get my attention. Normally, when I was working in the garden, I was oblivious to anything else. Black Eyed Susans, Purple Coneflowers, Butterfly Bushes; all would team together to shut my mind down from the outside world, creating a haven for me that I found difficult to leave. The dinner bell's intrusion reminded me that I could not escape forever. "Just a minute," I yelled back in return. It was hours before dinner, and the kids were swimming in the pool with Kelly. "What was it?" I wondered, as I walked down the path near the hosta bed.

Kelly's sheepish smile greeted me as I walked up to the pool. Everything was okay, the smile indicated to me, yet she must have had some sort of revelation to share with me. Avoiding Brody's cannonball splash, cascading water all about me, I steeled myself for Kelly's pronouncement.

"Hey, Boom. Mary called."

"Again?" I blurted out. Surely not another child!

"It's not that bad," she laughed, finding hilarity in my bowled over response. "She just wants us to look after Scotty's sister for this weekend."

A sigh escaped me, relief at Kelly's clarification. "Sure, no problem. When does she come?"

"Friday morning. She'll stay until Sunday afternoon. Here," she said, handing me the phone, "can you call Mary back and tell her its okay?"

"No problem," I answered, taking the phone in one hand, and gently pushing Kolby into the pool with my other. Squealing in delight, Kolby made sure to drench me with the largest splash she could muster up with her skinny frame. Grace was in a baby inflatable device, floating next to Jace, who was ever the caretaker of our family. Diving for toys on the bottom was Brody, while Scotty watched from the side. Though afraid in the beginning, Scotty loved the pool now, and took pride in the fact that he could jump into the deep end, fully preserved from any danger in his red and white body floating suit. The suit kept him wholly above the water, as he learned to paddle, grinning with his new set of teeth through each stroke. What was one more child for a weekend, I thought, as I placed the call to Mary.

I quickly learned what one more child was like. It wasn't a weekend; it was three years worth; at least that's what the three days felt like. Scotty's sister, Elizabeth, was only a year older than he, but they were like two different sides of the same coin, as opposite as they can be. Whereas Scotty was all smiles, 100 percent of the time, Elizabeth let everyone know that she was unhappy with whatever was occurring that moment. On top of that, she was one of those little generals who take charge of each moment, and each occasion; a prima donna already at age five. Perhaps it was the fact that she had not seen Scotty in some time. Perhaps it was the fact that she felt she needed to protect him. Whatever the reason, this five year old little pistol tried to be the parental figure with young Scotty, which often clashed with what Kelly and I were trying to do with him. She left us exhausted by the first night.

It was the Fourth of July that weekend, and we loaded up the kids into two cars that patriotic morning and headed over to Oxford, a small community thirty five minutes away from us. For years, now, we had taken our children to the town's modest Fourth of July parade. Our kids loved it, and we were happy to include Scotty and Elizabeth in the festivities. Through the blare of car horns, local politicians pressing the flesh, cowboys on horseback, and the required line up of four wheelers adorned in red, white, and blue streamers, the kids had a great time. Of course, the hundreds of pieces of candy thrown their way only brightened the morning for them, and we had to ensure that Elizabeth didn't fill her stomach with Jolly Ranchers and Sweet Tarts.

After a great deal of begging by our three older children, we allowed them to taste the thrill of adventure and go camping. Kolby, Jace, and Brody found great fun in camping at Disney World, and thirsted for that Daniel Boone experience again. So, I pulled out the tent from the basement closet, set it up in the front yard, and helped the kids get their sleeping bags, pillows, and plenty of blankets into their night time front yard suite. Scotty didn't last too long after it got dark before he wandered back into the house. Elizabeth, though, talked all night long, snuggled between Kolby and Jace. Brody was Brody, the single boy amidst a wave of girls; such was his life.

Sunday evening found Kelly and I drained of every ounce of parental energy we had. I felt like a worn and dirty shirt, limply thrown over a laundry basket. I was done in, and so was Kelly. Six kids were wearing enough. Elizabeth felt like six all by herself. We were more than happy to see her foster parents pick her up and take her back to their home. When they left, I closed the door behind me, threw Kelly a weary smile, and attempted an exhausted jig, as best as my done in body would allow.

A week later, Mary called to let us know that Scotty was leaving us, as he and Elizabeth were to be returned to their mother. Their older brother, though, would remain in his foster home, as the mother was still living with her boyfriend, Scotty and Elizabeth's father. Their older brother had been beaten severely by him on a number of occasions, and the mother was not willing to leave him, choosing instead the violent abuser over her own child. I shook my head in disgust and sadness by the news. Such sad stories, I thought, sad stories.

When Scotty left us, he wore his typical grandiose smile. We hugged and kissed him farewell, and waved goodbye as he left our driveway in the backseat of Mary's car. Scotty had brought to our home unbridled happiness and a joy for life that all instantly shared when they were around him. I was thankful for him in my life. At the same time, I was concerned for his future well being. It was becoming harder and harder to be a foster parent, it dawned on me that afternoon, as I reflected upon his re-unification with his mother. We take these children into our homes, make them a part of our families, love them unconditionally, laugh with them, shed tears with them, and watch them grow, only to see them return to a disturbing world. How much longer could we continue doing this?

CHAPTER 11

"**I** don't want to foster anymore."

Kelly stood in the kitchen, telling me this, shortly after Scotty left. She was preparing dinner, and I stood next to her, cleaning up the dirty dishes from the meal before. She had mentioned this to me before, after Sydney had moved to Florida, and I reminded her of it. "Hon, if we stopped fostering then, we would never have Grace come into our lives."

"I know, but I'm tired. Besides, I don't think we're good at it. The kids we take in deserve much better than us."

"Well, I understand..." I didn't really know how to respond further. I, too, was tired, but still felt called by God to continue. I was hoping, though, that God would allow us some time alone with the four children in our house. Besides, I was starting my doctoral work, and was hoping to focus on it.

Summer came to an end, and the new school year was upon us. Jace was in fourth grade, and Brody was beginning his year at a new school, as well, joining Jace at the primary school. Kolby was entering into middle school status, as she was now a sixth grader. I didn't want a middle school aged child. Too many complications, too much drama; at least, that's what I remembered when I was in middle school. Drama! I certainly had enough of it the past eight months to last for the next eight years.

Kelly's business was keeping her as busy as ever. She was also well into her first of three years as a serving elder of our church, and had taken the mantle of head of the Outreach committee. Add her doctoral work, and four children in our house, she was stretched thin. I felt the strain, as well. We were very much embracing having only four children in the house, and I felt like I could handle four with my eyes closed. It was so much easier with just our own.

Our own. Grace was not part of our own, just yet, at least not legally. That would happen in October, when the adoption officially went through. We were still nervous about it, as she was still in the custody of DFCS, and we both shared the fear that something might go terribly wrong. Perhaps something might block the adoption process. Perhaps a family member might come out of the woodwork and take custody of her. Perhaps the true birth father might rear his head and claim her. October couldn't come soon enough for the two of us.

Helena had enrolled in a brand new school in Macon, and continued to earn top grades. I was writing her letters every two weeks, giving her the latest news from our family, encouraging her to continue her great work in school, and reminding her of our love for her. About once a month, she would come to our house for a weekend visit, and our kids enjoyed seeing her.

Before we knew it, the fall weather swept into the state; the trees around our house were filled with yellows, oranges, and reds, corn was being harvested for the last time, sweet potatoes were dug up, and the summer flowers were fading. The kids took one last dip in the pool in September, shivering all the way back to the house. Life was full, yet we had fallen into a relaxed routine. It was time to take a little break from fostering, and recharge our batteries.

The call came again Tuesday night, the third week of September.

It was dinner when the phone rang, as we were in the middle of a meal, seated around the dinner table. I reached over the counter and picked up the phone, expecting anyone other than a caseworker.

"John, this is Cathy from DFCS. I hope I didn't interrupt anything."

My heart began to quicken, and I felt suddenly a little hotter under the collar in anticipation of what the call probably meant. Glancing at Kelly wide eyed, I whispered to her "DFCS!"

"No problem, Cathy. Always glad to hear from you. How can I help you?" I replied.

"John, I know that you and Kelly are hoping to have some time off from fostering, but we have an emergency where we need to place a child for a few days, until his uncle comes up from Florida to get him."

It seems that every time DFCS calls, it results in a heavy sigh escaping from me. I let out another, this time, before continuing. "Well....hmmm. How old is he?"

"He's thirteen, and he was found living under a highway overpass this morning a half hour away from y'all." THIRTEEN?!? Kelly and I had agreed that we wanted a break. More importantly, we didn't want to foster any child older than Kolby. This is NOT what I wanted to hear from Cathy. Sensing my reluctance from the silence on my end of the line, Cathy added, "I know y'all don't want any older children, and I understand if y'all say no. I just had to call and ask."

"Cathy," I said with uncertainty, "can I talk with Kelly and call you back?"

"Absolutely, John. Thanks."

"No problem. Thank you, Cathy; I'll call you back in a few minutes. Talk to you then." As I hung up the phone, I put my head down on the counter for a second, trying to digest what just happened. DFCS called. Again. They want us to foster a teenage boy. I'm so tired...

"Well...?" Kelly sat at the table, waiting for me to recover. I quickly repeated what Cathy had to say, and looked to her for an opinion. She frowned. "A thirteen year old boy could pose some real problems for our children. We don't know what he's been through, or what he might say. I'm worried that he might do something. I don't know, Boom, what do you think?"

"I agree; you're right. We don't know what he'll do or say. That's a tough age. But, it's just for a few days, like Cathy said. What do you want to do?" I asked. I wasn't real sure, myself, on how I felt about it.

This was a different situation, a tough decision. How would our own children be affected by this boy?

"I don't know," she paused, before adding, "let's pray." Holding the phone in one hand, I walked over to her, taking her hand in my free one. Once again, we looked to God for guidance.

After finishing, I asked, "Well, shall I call Cathy back and tell her... what?"

"Tell her we can do it," Kelly answered back, with a forced smile upon her face.

"Are we getting another foster child?" Kolby asked. Brody and Jace were listening carefully, while Grace was attempting to put food into her mouth.

"We are," I answered back, "and he's thirteen years old. He might be a little sad when he comes to us, so let's be really nice to him."

"We will," the chorus of children chimed back. Once again, I was thankful for the attitude my children had when fostering others. Many times, they, themselves, had been put through the wringer, and felt the sting of stress upon their young shoulders. Yet, each time DFCS called about taking another child in, my children were always ready to open their home.

T.J. arrived a half hour later after my phone call with Cathy. He was tall for his age, his brown ragged hair calling out for a haircut. His grey eyes told Kelly and me that he was not only distressed, but also scared. We welcomed him into the house with our warmest smiles, and soon had a plate of dinner and homemade cookies in front of him. Kissing our own children goodnight, Kelly and I sat down with Cathy in the parlor and filled out all the necessary paperwork. Cathy didn't have much to tell us about T.J.; he was with his mother under the overpass when located, he had only the clothes on his back, and most importantly, his birthday was in two days. As it was late, I made Cathy a cappuccino, and we bid her goodnight.

After a warm shower, T.J. sat on the couch in my borrowed pajamas, across from Kelly and I. The conversation was forced and awkward, and how could it not be. T.J. had been taken from his mother and placed in a home with strangers. His thirteen years made him very aware of his circumstances. Embarrassed and afraid, we did our best to put his mind at ease. The young boy's continuous yawning, though, told us that it was time for us to let him sleep.

The next day after work, I headed off to Macon to buy T.J. some birthday presents. Earlier that morning, I had enrolled him into middle school. Kelly had found out that morning over breakfast that T.J. used to own a skateboard. As he spoke of it, she could see the longing in his eyes, and decided to buy him a new one. It was another late night for me, as I arrived back home with a truckload of gifts for him. New clothes, shoes, a jacket, a few books, and his treasured skateboard; I had to run all over the city to find it, but I wasn't going to come home without it. Kelly had run to the grocery store during the day and had bought him a birthday cake. Though T.J. would be with us for a short time, we were determined to make it a special birthday.

When I arrived home that night, all five of the children were asleep, and Kelly was in bed, herself, working on her doctoral studies. I had been a little nervous throughout the day, leaving her alone with a teenage boy in the house. Kelly reassured me, rather quickly, as she told me that T.J. had been very eager to help around the house; cleaning up after dinner, folding clean clothes, and even holding Grace.

We awoke him the next morning with the DeGarmo traditional Birthday breakfast in bed. After school was over that day, we had a birthday meal with T.J., followed by him opening the presents. When he came to the skateboard, Kelly and I watched with anticipation, as he unwrapped it, and then breaking into the first smile since he came to us two nights before. In that short time, he had endeared himself to Kelly and my hearts. The next day, he left us, as relatives of his came to the school to pick him up during the middle of that day. T.J.'s time with us was short, though very pleasant.

My wife held Grace in her arms when I met her at the courthouse that Tuesday morning. Kolby, Jace, and Brody stood next to them, all dressed in their best church clothes. Amy was with them, along with Cathy and Nancy from DFCS. Surrounding them were a half dozen others, all coming to join in on the happy occasion. It was Adoption Day, and we were about to make Grace our own.

As I bent to kiss Kelly, I noticed out of the corner of my eye Grace's biological mother. I inwardly sighed, and asked God for my heart to soften. Noticing the surprise registered upon my face, Nancy quickly explained to Kelly and I that the mother was there to take part in her sister's court case. "Imagine that," I gritted between my teeth, "a little awkward, Kelly!" But, we had waited too long, and had worked too hard. We would NOT allow anything to spoil the event.

Within minutes, we were ushered into the jury deliberation room to sign the papers. Seated at the table were the judge and the state appointed lawyer, looking over the documents. As there weren't enough chairs for all of us, Kelly and I sat down, with the others circling the table.

"Good morning, I'm Judge Roberts," the older gentleman said, introducing himself.

"G'day, I'm Kelly DeGarmo," Kelly said, reaching across the table to meet his handshake. My heart pounded in the emotion of the moment, as I, too, introduced myself.

"Are all these people with you?" Judge Roberts asked, indicating to our supporters, crowding around us.

"They wanted to come and watch," Kelly smiled.

"In all my years doing this, I've never seen such a large turnout. This child must be rather special," the judge said.

"Oh, she is!" Amy quickly said, with a smile of her own. She was not about to miss this signing. After all, she had been adamant since the beginning that we adopt Grace. Now, the moment was almost at hand.

The lawyer read through the paperwork, and had us sign the necessary documents, with the judge signing his name to them, as well. Throughout this long process, the emotion of the moment brought warm tears to my eyes, and I was unashamed as they spilled forth, rolling down my cheeks. Seeing those tears, Kelly reached across and took my hand in hers. Her smile and tenderness only allowed the tears to continue, unabated. I let them flow freely, doing nothing to stop them; the adoption of this child was similar to child birth to me. I loved Grace Mariah DeGarmo as I loved my own children; no more, no less. There was now no difference between them, thanks be to God.

Finally, the paperwork came to an end, and tears were dried. Apparently, I wasn't the only one who had been crying; the room was filled with the sounds of sniffling and the passing of tissues. Sitting on Kelly's lap, Grace was oblivious to the commotion she was causing, as she played with Kelly's keys. All those people, all there to see her, and she didn't bat an eye.

"Well, Mr. and Mrs. DeGarmo," the judge grinned, looking at the two of us, "you two have done a wonderful thing in adopting this child. You are two very special people, and I thank you for what you have done for Grace. I can tell she is loved very much," he chucked to himself, as his hand swept across the room in gesture to the adoring crowd. "Do the two of you have any questions before we end today?"

Without hesitation, I looked him squarely in the eye, with a dead pan face, and asked him back, "Does this mean we can spank her whenever we wish to now?" The tension of the moment had been broken, and the room rang with laughter.

Puzzled, the judge sputtered, "Um...if you see fit to, I suppose..."

"Pay no mind to him, my husband can't help it," Kelly countered, almost by rote this time. Her response had become habit, and I burst out in laughter, myself. Kolby, Jace, and Brody only smiled, while Grace looked up from her keys, for just a moment, and smiled, too.

Standing back in the courthouse lobby moments later, we were showered with hugs and kisses from those who came to support us. Kelly and I took time to thank each of them in kind. Slipping a wrapped gift into Kelly's hand, Nancy gave her a hug and kiss on the cheek before turning to me for a hug, as well. I thanked her for all she had done the past year and a half.

After all had left, I kissed each of my four children on the forehead. Four children. All four legally ours. Then, placing Grace in Kolby's arms, I wrapped Kelly in an embrace from which I didn't want to leave. The stress of the past year and a half, the tension from court battles, the concerns of birth family members taking Grace away; all these vanished in the moment, melting away in my wife's arms.

The day was capped off with an Adoption Day celebration later on that night. It was a beautiful outpouring of people in honor of their love for our family and for Grace. Neighbors, church family, and friends from town all came, bringing trays and trays of food to eat, as well as gifts for Grace. It was the perfect way to end the day, surrounded by our extended family.

With the house cleaned up, dishes washed, and children finally in bed, I sank down in my own bed, next to Kelly. The emotions of the day had worn me out, and a good night's sleep was assured. Our hands intertwined, we lifted our praise for our dear friends and for Grace to God in prayer. Afterwards, she said, "Boomie, I was thinking tonight about fostering. It's hard for me to give up all of the other children. What about Sydney? What about Helena? You know, my heart still hurts over Mary Lou. It's so sad!"

"Mine does, too," I responded, lifting her hand to mine and kissing it. "I pray for those girls all the time."

"But what if it was our children; what if it was Kolby or Jace who were in a foster home? What if they were taken from us and placed in a strange home with a strange person telling them what to do? They would be so scared. Think about little Brody; what would he do if he were taken from his sisters and was all alone by himself in another home? He'd be nice and polite, saying "Yes ma'am," and "Yes sir." But, he would be so confused. Boomie, he'd be crying at night for his mommy and daddy. They all would be." I could feel her body tense next to mine, as the thought of our own children being placed in another home impassioned her.

"Thank God they're not," I tried to reassure her, without luck.

"And think of poor Scotty; he couldn't even talk. And what about his teeth? Boom, it's so sad," she repeated, sorrow drenching her every word. "Please, Jesus, take care of him and Elizabeth now, with their mother, and protect him."

"Amen," I said, grateful for her prayer. Like her, I shuddered at the thought of our own children in a foster home, and wondered if we were being good foster parents for the children that had come to us. More importantly, did I want to continue fostering? Many of our friends had said that they couldn't do it. Maybe we couldn't, as well.

As promised to Grace's biological mother, we had been allowing her to visit with Grace on occasion. Monticello was tiny, and we were bound to bump into her on occasion. Grocery store visits, trips to the library, banking; these were junctures where an unexpected visit might occur. It seemed better for all involved if we planned these visits, and one such visit was at the annual Haunticello that year.

Halloween has always been a favorite day of mine. When I was a child, I looked forward to the night of trick or treating just as much as I would Christmas. While December 25 held promises of Santa Claus and his presents, the magic of Rudolph and his flying peers, and snow covered days sledding down hills in Michigan, Halloween assured the first suggestions of the stage for me by dressing in costume, pillow cases full of every dentist's favorite candy, and a weekend around the classic horror films of a generation gone by, all in glorious black and white.

I first donned the mantle of "Pumpkinhead" back in 1989. It was my second year in college, and I wanted to wear something that was unique, yet harkened back to the spirit of the day at the same time. It was Andrew, a babysitter of mine when I was in elementary school, who first introduced it to me. Taking a large pumpkin, one that could cover his head, Andrew wore the pumpkin itself as a mask. By carving a hole on the bottom and then hollowing it out, the foreboding carving on the pumpkin, resting upon his shoulders, was an image that never left me. Except for my world travels with Up With People back in 1990, I have taken his idea and embraced it as my own each year. Curiously, large orange traditional American pumpkins were hard to find in Australia. Not to be defeated, though, I wore large watermelons, instead, on October 31. Two difficulties arose with this, though. First, Aussies do not celebrate Halloween, and I looked out of place during those years Down Under. Secondly, watermelons are simply that, a thin melon filled with water. Those Halloweens in my wife's native land found my head and shoulders drenched, yet undaunted.

So, when Halloween once again rolled around in fair Monticello in 2008, I was perhaps more excited than my own children were. This year, I could travel around the town's square with all four of my children, visiting the local merchants who were passing out candy to all of the ghosts and goblins during the annual two hour trick or treat event known as Haunticello. My children, and even Kelly, had become rather used to Pumpkinhead traveling alongside them, with my flowing purple cape and large pumpkin covering all evidence of my secret identity.

Before the collection of candy by the children and the gawking of young ghouls towards dear Pumpkinhead could commence, we visited with Grace's biological mother in the bank parking lot beforehand. It was the first contact between the two since the day of the court trial, and it was apparent that Grace was uncomfortable with it. Usually the child who would run up and give anyone a hug, she seemed awkward and distressed during the visit. Maybe she was simply ready for some trick or treating. Or maybe, she was simply ill at ease. It was difficult to watch her in this position.

November came, and along with it came Helena's eighteenth birthday. We drove to Macon and took her out to dinner, celebrating with her. Soon after that, Christmas came and went, this time with the Australian contingent of visitors, and we soon ushered in 2009. Even though we hadn't fostered any children for some time, we continued attending the foster parent association meetings every other month. The association, as it was called, was simply the foster parents in the county gathering together for additional training in all things foster care, as well as a foster parent support group. It was with this group where Kelly and I could fully be understood, where foster parents could appreciate what we had gone through, without telling us that we were crazy for fostering. They knew we were, because they were, as well. They, too, felt God's call to foster and had answered it. They, too, were absolutely dog tired, exhausted, worn out, and sleep deprived. My old friend from the original training sessions, Jason, had by now recognized my jokes for what they were, and joined in on them with some of his, also. We often shared grand laughs together, with both wives shaking their heads in dismay.

Kelly could now see the end in sight with her doctoral studies, and began a hard push to finish it. I, on the other hand, had only really begun, and was becoming rather excited about the topic. The course work required I do a lot of research about all things foster care, and I was fascinated by what I learned. I was not surprised to learn that foster children often exhibited both academic and behavioral adjustment issues, leading to high failure rates, dropout rates, and disciplinary problems. What I did learn, though, was that foster children often experienced multiple placement disruptions, and many schools often did not have the appropriate time to test a child for possible learning disabilities, prolonging possible assistance in that area for the child. It was disturbing to learn that, but explained a lot with some of the children we had seen in our house, or heard about from some of the foster families in our county.

The third Father Daughter Dance was even more successful than the previous two. As it was part of my vision to open it up to all in the town to attend, I invited a number of the churches to come along and join in and honor their girls, as well. Sure enough, many dads and their daughters from throughout the town came and celebrated the gift of our girls. Grace was in high form that night, as she discovered dancing. For two straight hours, she twirled, spun, jumped, hopped, and danced. By the end of the night, she was still spinning, though very slowly, with eyes closed, barely able to stand upon her two legs, yet, too stubborn to admit defeat. Kolby, Jace, and I simply watched from some chairs towards the end of the night, with us each taking a breather.

Spring was ready to burst out in bloom once more. Our home had not had a foster child for any significant amount of time since Scott left in July. As busy as we were with work, school, church obligations, and life in general, we felt relaxed, and the house was very much at peace. Four children was a breeze. So, God needed to shake things up a bit.

CHAPTER 12

We sat across Cathy in the parlor late that March night. It was around ten o'clock that Tuesday night, and both Kelly and Cathy were sipping on a cappuccino, while I held the four month old baby girl in my lap. Her four year old brother was asleep on the couch. It seemed that our family was about to be bumped up by two again.

The call came that afternoon, while Kelly and I were both at work. Cathy called Kelly and asked her if we would take in a four year old boy with his four month old sister. The children were to be removed that afternoon from their mother in a drug related case. Kelly called me and relayed Cathy's request. I was a little reluctant to take in a baby again so soon. After all, Grace was still in diapers, and I wasn't kicking up my heels to the thought of changing two diapers every morning. Yet, the call had been made, both by Cathy and by God. He was calling us to once again take more of His children into our house and care for them. I could hear some of my family members and friends in my ears, "John, don't do it. That's too many." Brushing this aside, Kelly and I quickly said a prayer over the phone, and I then asked her to call Cathy back, saying we would help out.

The night was a blur. There wasn't much information on the children, other than their ages, names, and birthdates. The baby continued to cry throughout the meeting with Cathy. Now, I had held many during the past ten years, and felt that I was an admiral in rank when it came to calming babies down. I had found just the right spot in the cusp of my forearm where many crying babies had found relief. Add to that my years as a performer, allowing me many different characters to perform and babies found me an Academy Award winning actor every time. Yet, Melinda was resisting all my efforts and to charm her into submission. Instead, she let forth in a howl like none I had ever encountered before. Crying as if in pain throughout the entire meeting, I tried every trick I knew to get her to stop, if even for just a minute. Kelly's attempts were futile, as well. I could tell that a long sleepless night lay ahead of us.

"Cathy, why are they in foster care?" Kelly asked, reaching over to place Melinda back in my arms.

"Mom is on meth, and doesn't have a job. We are looking for any family members who might want to take them in, but so far, we haven't found any." Cathy replied, with an exhausted smile.

"Is the dad in the picture?" I asked.

"No, he doesn't want anything to do with the children," she said, frowning.

We finished signing all the papers, and after gleaning all that Cathy knew, we thanked her for coming, and began taking the children to their beds for the night. Months ago, Brody had moved into Helena's old room, while Grace moved into his. As the room was the length of two rooms, we placed Grace's things on one end of the long room, and placed the sleeping boy on the other, in Brody's old bed. Earlier in the day, I pulled the baby crib out of a closet in the basement. As a foster parent, I found it necessary to keep many things stored away, as we never knew what age a child might be that came to us. Extra diapers, formula, a crib, toys, clothes, baby food, car seats, baby bouncers; all these were tucked away somewhere in the house, ready to come out when "the call" came. Kelly changed Melinda while I prepared a bottle for her. As Kelly had a busy day the next day massaging, I took duty that first night, placing the blonde haired baby girl in the crib which was set up in another room, outside the kitchen. As soon as I placed her down, she began to cry again. Crying wouldn't do it justice, though. This was a screamer. She kept screaming, shrieking, and screeching all night and well on into the morning. I assumed it was due to a new house environment for her, and that she was extra agitated.

The Mickey Mouse alarm clock next to my bed began clanging just moments after I laid my head down for the final time. It seemed as if

I had just shut my eyes before Mickey let me know that it was time to get back up again. I love Mickey, but I was a little frustrated with him this morning. I wanted more sleep. I NEEDED more sleep. As I lay there, attempting to gather the strength of Hercules required in order to move myself out of the bed, it hit me. The four year old boy's name, the one sleeping upstairs in my house; his name was…no, it couldn't be. I must have read it wrong.

Reaching the kitchen table, I thumbed through the papers we signed the night before. "Kelly, I think that Espin's name is spelled far different than we thought. I think it might be E..S..P..N, like the TV channel," I said, emphasizing each letter. Kelly was by no means a sports fan, at least an American sports fan, but she had seen me enough times in front of the channel, with my face painted green, and decked out in green and white from top to bottom, cheering on my Michigan State Spartans. I was one of those fans that deserved the fanatic label.

"I don't think so, check again," she replied.

"I don't know…." I said, scanning down the pages, looking for the spelling. "Yup! He's named after the TV channel, Kel. It's right here, E,S,P,N. He's named Espn."

"Are you sure? Maybe its spelled wrong on that page, check on another page," she said, unbelieving.

"Nope, it's spelled that way a few times," I replied, looking through the paperwork to check.

"Maybe DFCS spelled it wrong," Kelly said. "That's an unusual name." It was an unusual name, I thought, and DFCS did not spell it wrong, as I found out later that day, checking with Cathy. That evening, we found something else unusual about Espn. It was bath time, and the quiet young boy was being bathed by Kelly. It was the first time that either of us had an opportunity to take a good long look at him. The night before, it was late, and he was asleep. The morning found us hurrying around, getting all six children ready for school and daycare. Kelly took our four children in her car, and I rushed down breakfast and was out the door earlier than normal, as I had to register Espn and Melinda at the daycare center we use when we have foster children.

So, when Kelly was bathing Espn, she had the opportunity to closely examine him, and what she found was horrifying.

"Espn, how did you get this booboo," she asked him, pointing to the circular spots across his arms. At first glance, they looked to be round burn marks, fresh ones, at that.

"That's where my mommy put her cigarettes when I got in trouble." He said it so matter of factly, as if it was a common occurrence. As if it was common practice for all adults when punishing a child. Startled, Kelly soon began a thorough examination of Espn, looking for more.

"Espn, honey, did your mommy put cigarettes on top of your head, too?" She had noticed more of the small circular burn marks throughout his scalp.

"Yes," he said, unflinchingly.

"Did she do it anywhere else to you?" God, please no, thought Kelly.

"In here," Espn said, opening his mouth wide, and pointing to his tongue. Bending over the tub, Kelly peered into Espn's mouth. Yes, there were some burn spots on his tongue, as well. Quietly calling my name, as not to alarm the small four year old, I came in, holding the crying Melinda in one hand. Kelly pointed to the marks.

"Cigarette burns," she said, "from his mother. And they're on his tongue, too."

I groaned, as anger began to stir within me. How could parents be so cruel? I had had about enough of these gruesome stories about what birth parents did to their children. I stared at Espn a moment, feeling tenderness and compassion for what the young fella had been through, before returning to the kitchen and finished getting dinner ready.

Melinda continued her screaming assault that evening and long into the night before finally surrendering to exhaustion. It was Kelly's night to be on duty, though both of us got little sleep that second night. We awoke weary the next morning, and started our routine once again.

By the fourth night, Kelly and I were both dragging. Melinda had not ceased in her screaming. It did not seem to matter what we did, the four month old hollered out as if in pain every waking moment. Kelly and I tried to comfort her by rocking, hugging, and even holding her close. We tried to divert her attention with play and laughter. Feeding her did not bring relief, either for her or the two of us. She was quickly wearing us out.

Easter Saturday came, and with it, the church's annual Easter Egg hunt. This year, it was held at Mary Lou's house. Her glorious array of daffodils dotted her landscaped yard, making it the perfect site. Mary Lou, and her husband Jimmy, had been planting hundreds of daffodil bulbs throughout their yard for many years. This was THE place to be on a spring day. All of the children of the church gathered at Mary Lou and Jimmy's house that morning, with Easter baskets in hand. The night before, some church members had hidden hundreds of plastic Easter eggs throughout the yard. When all of the children had posed for a group picture, the word was given, and dozens of children dashed into the yard in search of their Easter treasures. Espn was right beside them, exploring between bushes and in between flowers, seeking out pink, purple, and yellow hollow eggs, filled with a plunder of sweets. Holding Melinda in my arms, I stood back and watched him, his blond hair waving in the gentle April breeze, his face lifted in a warm smile. It was good to see him laughing; laughing with other children his age and laughing with caring adults who were there to encourage and support him. He seldom laughed, having been through such horrors and terrors in his short four years. Laughter was indeed the best medicine, medicine he sorely needed.

Kelly had been talking with her good friend Shannon, our doctor, about Melinda's state. It had been over a month since the two came to stay with us, and the baby had not weakened any in her unremitting crying. What Kelly discovered was truly disturbing in its sadness for the little baby. Melinda was a Meth Baby.

According to the doctor, babies born to mothers addicted to meth generally suffer from a number of possible symptoms. Kelly explained to me that Melinda could suffer from brain damage, respiratory problems, neurological damage, organ damage, and general poor health. Kelly also informed that that Melinda's nonstop crying was probably due to the fact that the four month old was easily agitated, due to emotional problems, and would be this way for the rest of her life. Easily agitated; that would explain why she screamed, kicked, and fussed every waking moment. This tiny little baby suffered due to her mother's selfish need to take an illegal drug. Hearing this from Kelly only frustrated me. Again, I groped with the unanswerable question; how could birth parents treat their own child this way? I was angry with Melinda and Espn's mother and with many of the parents of the children that came through our home. It wasn't fair, it wasn't right, for parents to indiscriminately ruin the lives of so many innocent children. I struggled with this, as I felt I was being judgmental towards these parents. I had to remind myself that they, too, were children of God, and that He loved them just as much as He loved Kelly and I, my children, and everyone else.

The end of April brought another father/son baseball game at the local recreation field in town. Like the year before with Scotty, Espn managed to hit a home run each time he was at bat. How the fathers in the outfield continued to trip over themselves each time Espn came to bat was a mystery to me; a delightful and rewarding mystery. I thanked each of them, afterwards, for making it a special day for Espn, one of those rare days where a smile crossed his face.

We made another discovery about Melinda, this time towards the end of May. Cathy found out, by talking with the birth mother, that Melinda had tubes in her ears. After another doctor's visit, we learned that one of the tubes needed to be replaced. Apparently, this was also a cause for her constant discomfort, and we hoped that the tubes placed back in her ears properly would help to end the suffering, and perhaps finally bring a smile to her face.

It had been awhile since Sydney called our house, sending emotional shockwaves through our house. Kolby and Jace were old enough to remember Sydney, though Brody's memory of her was rather vague. The two older girls had mentioned her from time to time, wondering aloud how she might be. I, too, had not stopped thinking about her since last we spoke with her previous foster family. Unfortunately, we had lost the name and number of the family in Alabama. That spring, I was determined to track her down.

In May, I called up Cathy from DFCS. Cathy, like Mary with Helena and Scotty, had been a fantastic caseworker to work alongside with, and was so very helpful whenever Kelly or I had a question. Explaining a little back ground history of Sydney and our family, including the conversation we had with the family in Alabama, I asked her if she could contact some DFCS agencies in the neighboring state. After working on it, she called me back, with the unfortunate news that the state departments did not work alongside each other, and she, too met with a dead end. Disappointed, I next turned to searching for her via the internet, but again was met with no luck.

"Lord, I'm stuck. I have met with nothing but failure in looking for Sydney. God, I feel she's hurting, somewhere, and has nobody to help her out, nobody she can call family. Please guide me, open my eyes to how I can find her. Please point me in the right direction. Amen." Sending this prayer out, I waited for an answer.

It was summer time! Another season of pool diving, another season of gardening, and another season of being extra busy with camps, vacations, and even more school work for Kelly and I. Helena visited us often that summer, and we began to seriously talk to her about her future plans with college, and beyond. As she was a ward of the state, and still under DFCS' care, she would be eligible for college assistance, as well as housing aid. She was heading into her senior year, and we were excited for her, so many potentials.

It was official that summer. We became Disney Nuts, Disney Fanatics. After placing Espn and Melinda in respite with another foster family in a nearby county for a week, the six of us headed down to Disney World, once again. While we were there, we were joined by Kelly's mother, who had come over to visit for awhile. It was during this stay where we decided to join the Disney Vacation Club, which allowed us to come to the Magic Kingdom even more. It was at this point where I decided that we had lost it, officially. We had gone overboard. The two adults in the household loved Disney more than the four kids.

Something was off kilter with that. Maybe we needed to visit Disney more often to correct it.

Espn and Melinda's stay with the respite foster family proved positive, and the family fell in love with the two. They, too, had young children of their own, and felt called to foster. The break at Disney was not only enjoyable; it was a much needed break for us, as a family. Fostering Espn and Melinda was tough, and was quickly wearing our family down. Kelly and I felt completely exhausted each day. My legs were lead, my head was in a daze, my eardrums hurt, and my energy level was below zero. I was running on an empty tank before we went to Disney. Many were the days where Kelly and I barely made it through, before sinking into bed each night, dog tired. Add the cat in there, as well. We were all kinds of animal tired. The week away at Disney helped to relieve the two of us, at least for a little bit.

Yet, once back home, it seemed as if we hadn't had a break. Espn and Melinda were nonstop care. Melinda's crying had stopped a little once her tubes were fixed, but she still was highly agitated. Espn was learning to swim, and in fact, wore Scotty's red floating suit in his attempt at becoming Aquaman. His smile, though, never really came along. The two of them had been going to visitations once a week. Melinda was too little to know who her mother was. Kelly had become more of a mother by the time summer rolled around, as the two of them had been with us for a number of months. Espn, though, was different.

All of the foster children we had enjoyed visitations, at least when a parent, or both, showed up. Certainly, we had to pick up the pieces from the distorted truths told by many of them. But, Espn's visits were different. Each time he came home from seeing his mother, he was nonchalant, registering no emotion, whatsoever. No smiles, no tears; no happiness, no sadness. After months of this, Kelly's curiosity finally got the better of her.

"Espn, how was the visit, honey?" she asked one summer day, after the driver left.

"Okay," he said. It was his standard answer, never deviating from it.

Not afraid to push further, Kelly took it a step further. Bending down and resting her hands upon his shoulders, she gave him a kiss on the cheek and tussled his hair. Then, with a gentle smile, she went on. "Sweetheart, you just saw your mommy. Don't you like seeing your mommy?"

"No. My mommy hurts me. I don't like seeing her." It was the answer from a four year old boy who had been burnt and abused by someone. The tragedy, though, was that the person who inflicted such pain upon his tender, small frame was the one person in the world who was always supposed to protect him from such horrors.

Dismay registered upon Kelly's face, as her heart was wrenched from her by Espn's honest reply. Tears springing to her eyes, she pulled the four year old to her. Embracing him in her arms, the foster mother rubbed his back, kissing him gently on his forehead. "Oh, sweetheart......" What could she say? What were the right words for a four year old boy in this instance? Espn needed to hear something though, Kelly thought.

"Espn, you're going to be just fine. You are a very special boy, and many people love you. Jesus loves you, and we love you. I'm so sorry your mommy hurt you, but that isn't going to happen again, okay?" she asked, wiping the tear that was crawling down the left side of her cheek.

"Yes, ma'am," he said, standing there, with his arms at his side. Still, there was no smile; no emotion. He was as if a statue, perfectly still, unmoving.

It was towards the end of June when we received a call from Cathy letting us know that the family that had taken the two foster children into their homes earlier in the month, during our trip to Disney, had become very fond of the four year old and his baby sister. In fact, they were strongly considering adopting the two, as it was looking more and more likely that reunification between Espn and Melinda and their mother would not happen. For the next two weeks, Kelly and I spent a great deal of time on the phone with the foster mother, explaining to her in great detail all we could about the two foster children in our home.

With all the necessary paperwork out of the way, the second week of July saw Espn and Melinda leave our home for the new home, a permanent home, or so we hoped. As I dropped them off at the house, I was delighted to see that it was very similar to ours. The quaint country house was on plenty of land. There were animals abounding, a pool, and young children playing. Espn would feel comfortable in it, I prayed. Without much fanfare from either of the two children, I hugged them goodbye, and thanked the parents. Leaving the driveway and heading home, I asked God to bless the family, and prayed that Espn and Melinda's new home was the last stop for them. Moving from three different homes in four months is not healthy for anybody.

Multiple Displacements is a problem for foster children in foster care. A displacement occurs when a child is taken from his or her home suddenly, without warning, and placed in a foster home. When this happens more than once, it can be extremely traumatic for the foster child. I prayed this wasn't the case for Espn and Melinda.

Chapter 13

The house was empty again. Quiet reigned. At least, that's how it felt with only four children in the house. Melinda's crying no longer wore us down, and we didn't have Espn underfoot every moment, either. For once, we were pleased with the outcome of their departure. Not since Sarah and Mary Lou left had there been, what we considered, a happy ending. The two children had gone to a secure, loving, and stable environment with this new family, a family that was wishing to adopt them, and raise them as their own, much like we did with Grace. This knowledge made the transition much easier for us. We missed them, but were content that they were in a great place.

It was shortly after they left when Kelly made her request known to me, a request I had heard before. The kids were swimming in the pool, and Kelly was relaxing tableside, reading a book. I was outside the pool fence, deadheading some blooms from the numerous butterfly bushes that dotted the surrounding landscape.

"Boomie, I don't know if we should foster anymore."

Sighing inwardly, I continued deadheading, though turning my attention towards her as I took off the dead flowers from the large yellow butterfly bush. Butterflies, bees, and even hummingbirds filled the sky around me. I was tired from having six children in the house. At times, if felt like twice that amount. I had quickly accepted the fact that Espn and Melinda hadleft, and I welcomed a break. I understood Kelly's feelings, and part of me felt the same way. Yet, I still felt the call from God to continue opening our home to hurting children.

"I know, Kel. I'm tired, too. A break will do us good."

"I don't want a break, though. I don't want to do it anymore. I want to be done." Her voice was drained. "I know you don't want to be done, though."

"Well," I paused, thinking about just how I felt. I wasn't really sure. I certainly didn't want to foster more children at that moment. "What if we took a year off?"

"I don't know," she replied. "I don't think so. I want to take care of our own children. When we had Espn and Melinda, they took all of our time. Kolby, Jace, Brody, and Grace get lost in the shuffle any time we foster."

"But if we didn't foster, we wouldn't have Grace in our lives," I argued.

"I know," she said, exhaling softly. "And, I know that you like it. I know you think that we do a good job, and that the children are better off in our home. I just wonder if we are doing the right thing for foster children."

Summer ended, and with it began a new year at school. Kolby had taken up drumming the year before, when she first entered middle school, and was becoming quite proficient at it. As her bedroom was right under ours, often were the nights where Kelly and I heard every drumbeat and every tapping of the snare drum as she diligently practiced. Not wanting to discourage her, we put up with it. It felt like we were in the middle of the Tell Tale Heart; with its thumping like heart beat ringing through my head. Or, was it Poe's other classic, The Raven, with its knock, knock, knocking? Whatever story I was trapped in, it was deafening.

Helena announced that she was moving back to her parents' home after a year at the youth group home. Why I could certainly understand why she would not want to live in a group home, I was still puzzled. My puzzlement lay in the adults, her adoptive parents. After having her in their home for six years, abusing her along the way, they had given her back to the state, where she was delivered to our home, delivered by God. Then, after some very difficult sessions with the psychiatrist, shortly before we were set to adopt her, they told her that she was no longer part of their family. But, after a year at the group home, they wanted her back. Something wasn't right, and Kelly and I were concerned. Helena bolted to the head of my prayer list, and I continued writing her letters every two weeks, encouraging her and reminding her of God's love for her.

The next few months flew by, and the Yuletide season of Christmas quickly fell upon us. We were busy with the traditional events of the season, but the hectic schedule did not tire us in the least. Once again, it seemed like a breeze with only our four children in the house. Grace was now three years old, and not in diapers. Not in diapers! It had been some time since I hadn't changed a diaper. It was a Christmas miracle!

Grace was a miracle, though; a miracle for our family. This little child, who could fit in the palm of my hand the day she arrived to our home, only five days old, had been a blessing to all who lived in our home. Grace's spirit and sense of adventure often consumed our other children, as well. I was quite curious how she would deal with the skin color difference, though. Society would call her "black," while her siblings and parents would be labeled as "white." Kelly and I, though, had taught our children from the beginning that there is no difference in skin color, and that all people are just different shades of God's skin. The old Up With People song, "What color is God's skin?" was a powerful one. When we sang it on stage, all those years ago, in front of thousands, the words always were fresh ones, never growing stale through countless performances. "It is black, brown, yellow, red, it is white. Everyone's the same in the good Lord's sight." Though Up With People was by no means a Christian organization, the words of that song rang true to so many who heard it, and it was one of their most requested songs. I didn't see Grace as a "black" person, as I did not see my birth children as "white." In fact, I didn't see any difference between them, as the love I felt for all four of them was equal.

One day, when Grace and I were at the grocery store, waiting in line, an older lady was in front of us. As is often the case, when I am with Grace, we were being stared at, no doubt due to the color thing between her and I. I could feel the lady's stare bearing down upon us. Turning to her, I smiled. As I did so, she returned my smile.

"She's so purty. That baby girl is right purty." Pausing, she then asked what was on her mind. "Is she African American?" Her voice was like a semi trailer; loud - get out of my way loud - or I'll run you over loud. Her color was similar to Graces', and she was probably wondering why I was holding such a cute looking "black" baby.

Without hesitation, my answer slipped right out of me, as if it was rehearsed. "No, ma'am, she's Australian American."

Now, I'm pretty sure this lady may have been prepared for many things, but it was apparent that this was a response that she didn't expect, or, for that matter, probably had never heard before. She sputtered, stammered, hummed, and hawed; confused in every manner. "...uh.... Wha? ..." And then it came, for the seven surrounding check out lanes, and entire east wing of the produce department to hear. "Did YOU say AUSTRALIAN American? Is that what you said?"

I was enjoying this. "Yes, ma'am. Australian American. Her mother is Australian and her daddy is American," I said, tilting my head with a smile.

She looked Grace up and down with a quizzical gape in her eyes "Oh.....oh.....oh..." And then, very feebly, "um...that's nice." It seemed that the conversation was over, even if I wished to explain further, as the older lady began to examine everything that might be at her feet, with an intensity that I wished the Michigan State basketball team would bring to every game.

Kelly and I had not had a vacation together for some time. In fact, with four plus children in the house, we seldom had a moment to ourselves. So, it was with great surprise when she took me to Disney World for my birthday during the New Year's holiday. Just me! O, how glorious. No diapers to change, no children waking me up in the morning waiting for breakfast, no children arguing with each other because one was looking at another. The two of us could have a discussion by ourselves without being interrupted within three minutes.

I could eat ice cream without feeling guilty about making sure there was enough for four little mouths. O, how wonderful!

Once again, the forsythia bloomed, the daffodils burst forth, and the blue birds returned to the numerous bird houses in our yard. Spring sallied forth, and with it, Kelly's graduation. She was now officially Doctor DeGarmo. As was typical of her, she wanted no fanfare, no ceremony, and no recognition. I, on the other hand, was quite proud of her, and wanted to sing forth the news. After all, she had undergone a grueling course load to become a doctor of natural medicines, a naturopathic doctor, all the while raising our four children plus a host of others, serving as an active session member at church, and running her own business. I knew how hard she had worked for this, and realized that she could have quit long ago, with the many obstacles before her, as well as all the responsibilities on her plate throughout. Her new degree completed, she began to consult others about their diet as well as continued in her massaging. It had been two years since Kelly had been to Australia. She was anxious to get back to her homeland, and Shirley was even more anxious to see her grandchildren. So, with summer coming up, we decided that early June would be the best time for the family to take the long trip to the land of kangaroos and koalas. When we booked the tickets, there was some question about me going, for two main reasons. First, I was considering applying for an assistant principal's position at another school, and we were unsure if I could take such a long time off if offered the position. Along with that, the course I was taking that semester required that I had the first section, or chapter, of my dissertation completed. Somehow, spending two thousand dollars for my ticket to fly to Australia, simply to spread out mountains of articles over my mother in laws table while spending two to three hours a day on the chapter didn't fill me with visions of dancing sugarplums.

Two days after school finished for the year, Kelly was on a plane with the four children, leaving me at home for the next three weeks. Thankfully, this trip was not a repeat of the last time she took three children by herself to Australia, in the spring of 2001. That trip, Kolby and Jace had the distinct pleasure of vomiting seven times between them while on board the plane bound to Sydney. Brody was just nine months at the time, Jace a year and a half, and Kolby not yet four. Lugging all three small ones back to the plane's tiny bathroom each time, Kelly attempted to rinse the vomit from their clothes and dry them, as all of their clothing and belongings were under the plane, in the suitcases.

"Oh, honey, that's terrible," I said when my crying wife called upon landing in Sydney, relaying to me her flight of horror. "I wish I could have been with you to help out." Actually, I was quite glad I WASN'T there to share in a vomit filled flight. Somehow, that thought didn't fill my head with sugarplums, either. I would have cracked under the pressure, like a jailbird grilled in the good cop bad cop back room interrogation scene.

I spent those three weeks hard at work on my dissertation, and was able to hammer out the first section, spending about five hours a day on it. Along with this, I spent the remaining hours in the garden. To my surprise, I did not enjoy the time alone as much as I originally thought I might. Whereas I suspected the quiet house would be a peaceful one, it ended up being an empty one, too empty for me to truly appreciate. I missed the kids, and I missed Kelly. The three weeks dragged by before we were all reunited. Whoever sang the song about reuniting was spot on the money when they suggested that it felt so good.

For over a year now, I had been encouraging Helena to attend college. I saw so much potential for her future, a future that would be brighter with a college degree. Yet, I was concerned that she would choose not to go, and tragically squander the wonderful brain that God had given her. Sadly, her adoptive parents were telling her the opposite, that college was not important, and that she need not go. The environment she was in was a harmful and destructive one, and I feared that she would be sucked into it, continuing on heartbreaking cycle.

Helena did want to go, though, despite those who wished otherwise. Working with a DFCS employee, she decided upon a college an hour away. When it came time to enroll, though, her family was nowhere to be seen, they would not help her register for her classes, nor even visit the campus with her. Again, Helena had no one to fight for her, to stand up and guide her through the maze of challenges that life threw at her.

The young Romanian was part of my family, and I offered to visit the campus with her, and help her with the enrollment process. As Kelly was still in Australia, I drove up with Helena to the college, and played the part of a parent, helping her register, enroll for classes, and all that came with sending off a child to college. As I drove home that day, pleased with how everything turned out, it dawned on me; when you foster, you foster for life. These children are always going to be a part of our lives; they will always be family, no matter the circumstances.

It had been twenty years since Kelly and I had traveled with Up With People. It had been twenty years since we had first met. It had also been twenty years since we had seen many of those we traveled with. There was a handful that I stayed in contact with. The others, I was most curious about. That year, 1990, was a life changing year, it helped shape me into who I became, and I missed many of those I traveled with. Kelly felt exactly the same.

Twenty years; it seemed a long time ago. We had been through a great deal during that time. The death of our first child; living on an island; moving to the States; working in professional wrestling; having three children; adopting Grace; lots of college; and lots more foster children. So, when we heard about the twentieth anniversary being held in Arizona the last weekend of July, we immediately booked plane tickets, hotel reservations, and my mother as a babysitter.

Yet, as Kelly and I were walking through the hotel lobby to our room shortly after we arrived, hands intertwined, I became a little nervous. It had been twenty years. That WAS a long time. I hadn't seen these people since that tearful night in Sweden, when we all went our separate ways and separate nations. It was among one of the most emotional nights of my life, filled with great sorrow, saying goodbye to the dearest friends I knew. Would I be able to recognize them? Would I remember their names? Would they know who I was?

Those very thoughts were creating a wrinkled brow on my forehead when I heard a familiar voice. "So, are you two just going to walk by and not say hello to me?" Standing there, with a grin as big as the state he was from stood Terry, Terry from Texas. Last time I saw him, he did not have a beard. Other than that, he looked the same.

"TERRY!" Kelly screamed in joy, rushing to hug him. As I did the same, I noticed a half dozen other Uppies, how Up With People cast members referred to themselves. They began rising from the couch to greet us, and suddenly all the names were coming back to me. Shannon, Ed, Abbi, Tim, Jay, Jason. We had only walked into the hotel moments ago, and my concerns about memory lapses swiftly flew by as fast as the roadrunners I saw while riding in the taxi. Like two teenagers, Kelly and I dashed to our room, threw our suitcases on the bed, and ran to meet the others at lunch. I felt like a kid running down the stairs on Christmas morning, ready to tear into the presents waiting for me under the tree. This time, the presents were waiting for both Kelly and I in the hotel restaurant.

The rest of the day was filled with much of the same, meeting up with old friends. Night came, and we were blissfully exhausted. But, like those giggling teenagers, neither Kelly nor I wanted to go to bed, we were afraid we were going to miss something. It was well after three AM when we hit the pillows, but we weren't ready to succumb to the Sandman just yet. The two of us laughed long into the morning, reminiscing together about 1990, and sharing our view and opinions of the day.

The next morning, we both rushed to breakfast, looking forward to spending the day with old friends. At one point in the afternoon, we all gathered together, and played catch up, learning what each had been up to the past twenty years. Many had not heard that Kelly and I were married, while some others had heard through the years, but didn't consider it true. I didn't know whether to be insulted by that or not. Probably better I don't know, I thought to myself.

My nerves started racking again when we began rehearsing some portions of our two hour show for a performance later that night.

"Tim, I don't know if I remember the songs," I half jokingly told him. "It's been a long time."

"Aw, come on, Boomer, you'll be fine," he laughed. He didn't seem to notice that I wasn't laughing. Or, maybe he thought it was funny that

I was verging on a collapse of minor proportions. I was concerned that I would get on stage and make a complete fool of myself in front of the few thousands who would be watching. Now, I didn't mind making a fool of myself in front of others. I did it on a daily basis, and I often enjoyed it. But, this....this was a little different. When it came time to perform in front of others, I took it quite seriously, and felt the sting of every little mistake like a bullet from the musical assassin. I looked around the room for somewhere to hide, but couldn't find any avenue for escape. All around me were Uppies smiling, laughing, and singing. Kelly offered no life line, as she sat next to Chris from Canada, ignoring my mental pleas for help. Heck, Vito was even doing back flips. At age forty.... something! And, Taija, who had flown all the way from Finland, was doing her dance routine from the show. The rest of us all stood back, mouths wide enough to allow the Arizona flies room to fly around in.

My concerns, though, vanished as soon as we hit the stage, and sang our five songs. Suddenly, it was as if no time had passed. Chris, Andrew, Mo, Tina and I were on the microphones, while there stood Tim, Jason, Julia and the others, standing and dancing next to Kelly. The lump in my throat threatened to jump out and smash into Chris, while the tears running down my face were certain to soak Andrew. It was an electric night, it was a spectacular weekend, and   I didn't want to leave.

But, the weekend did end, and we did have to leave. As Kelly and I got into the car at the Atlanta airport, I turned the key with one hand and popped a Best of Up With People CD into the CD machine with the other. The drive home had us both in tears, as we sang along to the music at the top of our lungs. Something special had happened to me those three days away, to both of us those three days. The weekend had touched something inside me that I thought was dead and buried. More than that, the reunion with these people reminded me of who I was, and who I had become. I didn't like the former. I realized that I had forgotten my global roots, my desire to travel, and my desire to reach out to others around the globe. My cup had been refilled and replenished, as if I was reawakened after a long sleep. Both Kelly and I were all smiles for the next few weeks; our children noticed, those at church noticed, and my colleagues at work noticed. There was so much joy spilling out of me, and I felt like a different person.

Coming home, the two of us realized that we both wanted to experience another reunion, this time in Europe. So, we began to plan a European reunion with those Uppies who couldn't make the trip to the States and to Arizona. This time, the reunion would take place in the summer of 2011, in Switzerland. The difference, we would take our children with us.

The next few months went by quickly. A trip to Disney World again in October, continued work on my dissertation, and even Jace in middle school. Life was full. Then, one day in early November, we got the call again.

"Hey, John, this is Cathy from DFCS, I hope I didn't interrupt you."

"No, never, Cathy it's great to hear from you," I said, as I took my plate to the kitchen. We had just finished dinner that Thursday night, and were just relaxing around the table for a few minutes.

"Listen, Patsy and Mike are going to need a home for their three foster children for just three days, while they are away. There's three of them; a four year old girl, and her two brothers; ages 2 and a six month old. Do you think you and Kelly can take them?"

"Well, let me check, Cathy. Can you hang on a minute, while Kel and I talk about it?"

"Sure, of course!" she said. I quickly relayed the message to Kelly, and after a prayer, we both came to the same response; we would be happy to help Mike and Patsy, two foster parents in our town. We had grown fond of the two during the foster parent association meetings we attended. After all, how bad could three days be?

The three days did go smooth. Our three new arrivals came Sunday afternoon, after church. Mike and Patsy brought them over, along with two car seats, two cribs, plenty of diapers, clothes, and baby formula. Buried under all the items were three smiling children. Well, make that two smiling children. The baby, Jack, had become a "Mama's Boy," as he was very attached to Patty. Kelly and I had noticed this earlier, at a foster parent meeting. In a way, it was sad; sad that this young boy had grown to know Patsy as his mother, instead of his biological mother. Reunification would be hard for the baby and for Patsy.

Kolby and Jace instantly fell for the two boys, as they mothered and cared for them. Jack's crying ended soon after Mike and Patsy left, and the other two, Daniel and Ami, soon were running around, giggling and laughing with Grace. Brody wasn't too impressed, though. Once again, he was stuck with more babies and girls in the house, and no one to play with.

Wednesday morning came, and with it the departure of the children. It had been the easiest fostering experience we had had. Sure, Ami was a handful, with her "potty mouth" and constant chatter, but nothing that we couldn't handle. My initial concern.….no, my initial Fear had been that seven kids in the house would be too much. It was just the opposite, and Kelly and I felt good about it. All four of ours had stepped up to the plate and had hit another homerun. Without them, Kelly and I would have been overwhelmed with diaper changing, feeding, washing, and all that came with three extra children in the house.

"I felt good about that, Kelly, it was a good experience. We can do three kids," I told her, shortly after Mike had stopped by after work to pick up the children's belongings. I did feel good. I felt like we handled it rather easily. I could do seven kids. Little did I know that our hardest challenge lie just ahead.

CHAPTER 14

"Hi John, its Cathy." I was always glad to hear the DFCS case supervisor's voice, as it was a pleasure to work with her. After all, she laughed at all my jokes.

"Hey, Cathy!"

"How did it go with Mike and Patsy's kids?"

"It went great! I was a little worried about it, but we had no problems. I was telling Kelly that I think it was the best fostering experience we have had in a while. I even told her that we could do seven kids."

"That's wonderful. I'm glad to hear it. Speaking of that..." She hesitated. Uh-oh, I thought. This just wasn't a pleasure call, or a call to see how we were doing. I braced myself. Ami, Daniel, and Jack had only been gone for one day, and I certainly wasn't expecting a call so soon, if this was indeed THE call.

Taking a deep breath and then exhaling, I prepared myself. "What's up?" Kelly stood nearby, waiting to see where the phone call might lead.

"Well, we took three children into custody today. I know it's just been a day since the other three left, but I wonder if y'all can take these new ones."

"Ah....you better speak to Kelly about that, Cathy." I handed the phone to my bride. Kelly had said on countless occasions that she was done fostering. If we were going to do this, it had to be up to her.

Trying my best to piece the conversation together based on what Kelly said, I stood next to her, unmoving, lest I miss something. Finally, after numerous questions on her side, the phone call ended. Turning to me with the tiniest trace of a smile upon her face, she let out a slight sigh, her shoulders rising and falling in an attempt to relax.

"Well," I said, anxious to know all the details about our potential new family members, "what did she say?"

"There are three kids, and they're all in diapers. The oldest boy is three, his eighteen month old brother, and a four month old sister. She doesn't know how long they'll be in, but it could be a while. Their mom is working hard on doing what she has to do, Cathy said, in order to get them back."

"You know, this morning when I was doing my devotions, I read the scripture verse from Matthew 25:35, which said 'For I was hungry, and you gave me something to eat; I was thirsty, and you gave me something to drink; I was a stranger, and you took me in.' Maybe that was God's way of telling me that we can do this. After all, it went really well this past week with the other three."

"Let's pray," she simply said.

Taking her hand in mine once again, I prayed aloud. "Dear God, we thank You for the opportunity to serve You in fostering. We thank you that all went well with the three this week. Lord, we don't know if You would have us take these there into our home. We need some sign that this is Your will for us. You know how wearing this can be on our family, but we want to serve You in all we do. Thank You for our many blessings. We love You, Lord, and thank You for Your love for us. In Your name, we pray. Amen."

"Boomie, what should we do?" I could see the answer was already inside her, though she was looking for me to affirm it.

"It's what we do. We're DeGarmos; we foster," I said, a smile forming around the corners of my mouth.

"Okay, I'll call her back," Kelly said, with some anticipation in her voice, as she picked up the phone to let Cathy know that we were ready. I was only a little surprised that she agreed to take the three in. After all, she had said that she was through fostering. Yet, as I had pointed out to her, as well as to Cathy and Mary, every time DFCS calls, she gives in. Kelly's compassion is overwhelming towards others, as she always puts others' needs before hers. At times, this has been problematic for her, as she slowly wears herself down to the point of exhaustion, usually when we have foster children living amongst us. It can be both physically and emotionally draining, and Kelly often takes the brunt of it, as the children gravitate to her motherly love and mothering instincts.

I was sitting in my office at work the next day at lunch when Cathy called. The children would be arriving at our home around three that afternoon, instead of the weekend, as first planned. After getting some more information from Cathy, I immediately called Kelly, leaving a message on her machine. My heart started racing in anxiety, as my mind rapidly put together a list of what needed to be done beforehand. A bed, an extra crib, food, diapers, baby formula, car seats; the list seemed daunting, and I began to tense some in the shoulders. Asking for the remainder of the afternoon off from work, I raced around town, zipping from one place to another, before hurrying home to prepare the house. It was two in the afternoon when I arrived home. Our own children would not be home until another two hours, which gave me one hour uninterrupted to set everything up before the three arrived. After putting away the diapers and food away, I set up the cribs and took the baby bed out of Grace's room, placing in into another room in the basement, between Brody's room and the library. The guest room, which we had refurnished the month before, would be for my parents, who were coming for Thanksgiving, and then for Shirley and her sister, Trish, who were flying over to America to spend two months, arriving the day after my parents left. Full didn't begin to describe how the house would be the next few months. My neck and head began to ache just thinking about it.

Lisa, a caseworker who worked at DFCS, called soon after I arrived to let me know that she would be bring the children by after four that afternoon, as some unforeseen problems had arisen. By the time they arrived, Kelly and the kids were already home, and were able to help out with the transition. Kolby and Jace took the two older boys upstairs to their room with them, giving Kelly and I time to talk with Lisa alone. The baby crying loudly, Kelly and I did our best to quell her agitation.

With a look of exhaustion, Lisa gave us all the information she knew. The boys had been beaten by their mother with an electrical cord. The oldest boy, Micah, and his sister Linda, both shared the same father, who was in jail. The middle child, Joshua, had a different father, who was nowhere to be found. Sadly, Kelly and I found this to be typical; different fathers who chose not to be involved with their children. The mother was only a child herself, a young twenty one year old. After some calculating of my own, I determined that she was around seventeen when she first became pregnant, which I also found disturbing; children having children. It was a cycle that tragically often repeated itself. It was a cycle that I found was seemingly tough to break, and it was one of the reasons we fostered.

The night was difficult, one of the toughest I had had as a foster parent. The common first night traumas were magnified by three this night. Micah, Joshua, and Linda all cried, and each cried in a different fashion. Micah's cry was one of sadness, as he came to realize that he was not to be returned to his mother that night. A scream unlike any other heard in our house came from Joshua, a scream which contained great anger in it. Linda's cry was one of a tired and fussy infant.

I went to Micah's bed and tried to comfort him best I could. Brushing back his hair and wiping away the tears that rained down freely, I attempted to comfort him, failing in my attempt, as his crying lasted well into the night, as he cried himself to sleep. His crying was uncontrollable, and his despair hung about him. His sadness was tremendous, and I felt it keenly, as if he were my own child. I could feel the blush of frustration begin to boil within me, as I felt frustration towards his birth parents for placing him in this position, of being placed in a foster home. This young boy had done nothing to deserve the trauma that overwhelmed him. He was only three years old; how could loving parents do this to a child? Once more, I was frustrated towards those who brought him into the world, those who supposedly loved him most.

As I tried to soothe Micah, Kelly faced the tears of the other two. With Linda in one arm, she attempted to stop Joshua's outburst. The high pitched scream that roared forth from his small lungs soon unnerved both Kelly and I. His body shuddered with rage, as he shook the crib with all his might. So strong was his explosion of fury that he shook the crib from one side of the room to another; the crib literally moving across the floor. Like Micah, Joshua's crying did not fade quietly into the night. Instead, it lasted for well into the night, until he, too, dropped into a slumber from exhaustion. As for little Linda, a bottle quickly pacified her, and she was sleeping like the baby she was. By the time Kelly and I slid between the covers, it was well past midnight. Sleep did not come quickly to the two of us, though; the night's events were too fresh in our minds.

Normally, Grace is the first up in morning. As she knows that Daddy and Mommy are still sleeping, she is graciously quiet, careful not to disturb her slumbering parents. Joshua did not share this consideration, my wife and I found out. With just the slightest hint that the world was waking for another day, Joshua informed our home that he was rather unsatisfied with his current condition and location. Repeating his actions from just a few hours ago, his shrieking and shaking of his crib soon had me out of bed, springing to see what might be the matter. His face was contorted in anger, anger that should not have been harboring in such a small frame. I was taken aback; as it was something I was unfamiliar with.

With Kelly off to work that morning, I had my hands full with the three new ones. Joshua was demanding in his anger, and Micah was in no way potty trained, I found out quickly. For someone so small, his bladder was tremendous. The little three year old needed to have his diaper changed from a bowel movement six times that day. We were to find out in the next few weeks that six times were by no means a lot. He hit eleven bowel movements one day, a record I never wanted to be a part of, in any record book.

I quickly found out the following day, while driving to church that the Volkswagen bug I had been driving back and forth to work for a number of years was going to have to go, and quick. The car was simply much too small to fit three car seats in the back seat. We were now a two car family, whenever all of us should leave the house. With nine of us under the same roof, it was time to buy the "FosterMobile,"

I jokingly told Kelly. After school, Monday, I met Kelly at the local car dealership, and we soon found a new car to replace the VW.

Micah eventually settled down at bedtime each evening. Joshua was a different manner altogether. His shrieking remained consistent, as he bellowed forth in anger when put to bed. School mornings were even more difficult. Getting four children ready for school was hectic enough, the addition of three more in diapers was more than challenging, and it bordered on bedlam. Our house resembled a circus, with Kelly and I acting as dual ring leaders. Micah needed bathing each morning, as he would soil himself so thoroughly and so completely. There were a few mornings where his pajamas and bed sheets had to be thrown away. Joshua was his usual cranky self when awoken, while Linda was a typical four month old baby, a handful. Thus, it was with three children that needed bathing and diaper changing each morning, as well as the other four. Add Kelly and I, who both had to get ready for work ourselves, and it was a scene right out of a comic strip.

Thanksgiving came and with it, the first of our visitors; my parents and sister, who stayed with us for a few days during the holiday week. When Turkey Time ended, my parents returned back to Michigan, and Shirley arrived to take their place. A few weeks later, her sister Trish came to join us. Now, Trish had not fully entered into our family yet. She had never been to Disney World. This fact was highly disturbing to Kelly. How could her Aunt Trish relate to our family? Even more so, how could Trish continue to face each day? She needed help, and it was up to Kelly to provide this Australian the type of aid that only the Magic Kingdom could provide.

Kelly, Shirley, Trish, and Grace left Sunday evening, immediately after the town's annual community Christmas concert. I was happy to see them drive off, yet I had some concerns. First off, I was concerned for the travel. The eight hour trip was a long one for Kelly, and I prayed that they would be surrounded by God's hand while driving there and back. My second concern lay in the fact that....I was the ONLY adult in a house of SIX children. I was not only concerned, I was downright scared, scared for my life!

The house quickly became an assembly line the following Monday. While Kelly and her crew waited in lines at Disney, there were lines forming in our house, as well. There were shifts for the bath, for dinner, for story time, and for bed. The mornings were similar, as I tried to juggle the three babies. I soon found a new appreciation for single parents, and was grateful for my three children, as they helped out, each in their own way. Brody would play with Micah, Kolby and Jace would help out with feeding the two boys, and all were determined to feed little Linda a bottle. It was with relief that I met Kelly at the door Friday afternoon, when they returned. I had survived, though barely. A friend of mine once told me that I was to never have the children outnumber the amount of adults in the house. I saw the logic in this age old proverb.

Christmas day was wonderful, as it always was in our house. This year, though, it was often interrupted with diaper changes. By this time, we had found out that Micah had problems with his bowel system, according to his caseworker. Though I was no doctor, I pretty much had that one figured out, already. Kelly and I were determined to potty train the young three year old, for his benefit, and ours. As for presents that day, no one was happier with their gift than I was, with my very own concertina, or small accordion. I bought it for myself back in October, but waited for Christmas day to unveil it to the family. I had wrapped it up in a large box, and placed it under the tree, putting Shirley's name to it. I sure did love Santa that year.

I pulled into Robert's yard to pick him up early that morning. In the back seats were Grace, Micah, Linda, and Joshua. Robert was a student at the school I worked at, and we were taking him to church with us that Sunday morning as a guest. I was happy to see him, and greeted him with a handshake and smile. My smile though, soon rapidly turned into a nervous grin, ala carte, my daughter Grace.

"Children, this is Robert. Robert, this is my daughter Grace, and my three foster children, Micah, Joshua, and Linda," I said, as he buckled his seat belt.

"Hey, Daddy, Robert's brown like me," the newly turned four year old pronounced for the whole car to hear. She had recently discerned that her skin color was a little different than her mother and father's. My skin color, at the moment, was bright red, in embarrassment and surprise.

"Um......" I wasn't sure how to respond to this. Robert sat next to me, smiling. "Uh....that's right, he is." I turned to the high school junior, and tried to explain, as awkwardly as I could. "Robert, Grace is discovering that her skin color is not the same as mine. Gracie," I then asked, looking in the rear view mirror at her beaming smile, "what color am I?" I was curious to know, would she label me "white"?

"Silly daddy; you know what color you are." She folded her arms, and gave me that look, that look that said I was playing with her, that look that indicated that she was much older than four.

"Well, what color IS that, sweetheart?"

"Daddy, you're yellow," she replied, straight faced. Out of the mouths of babes.....

We had been having some problems on visitation day with the birth mother. To begin with, we had asked the driver, as well as the caseworker, to please see that the children ate healthy during the visits. When they first came to us, it was apparent that the boys suffered from malnutrition, cookies and sugary juice being their staple diet. Our requests were met with deaf ears, as the boys were fed "junk food." The problem lie in the fact that they were not only high strung those visitation nights, they also became sick, which by no means helped Micah in his diaper adventure.

Micah's hair was also in need of a desperate hair cut. In fact, the young three year old was a hair disaster. Not only did we want to take him to the barber's for a hair cut for the simple benefit of appearance's sake, it would also benefit Kelly and I in the mornings when his hair was full of urine and his nightly explosive diaper adventures, which would leave him covered. Again, the mother refused to allow us this luxury, even though it was repeated to her weekly.

The letter from the birth mother, though, was the most disturbing. As the children's driver left our house, after dropping off the children one evening, she handed a note to me, telling me that the mother had a few things she wanted to tell us. After getting the children bathed and fed, I took a look at the letter. It certainly wasn't a letter of thanks or gratitude for what Kelly and I were doing. Instead, the birth mother proceeded to let us know how we could be better parents to her children, as she listed all of the things we were doing wrong for her children. Unable to really appreciate the content of the letter, I re-read it. Still a little shocked by it, I read it yet a third time. Each reading of it only increased my disillusionment. Once again, I was being cast as the bad guy in all of this, the evil foster parent. My head told me that this was normal, and that I had gone through this before. My heart, though, was telling me another thing. I was more than a little disappointed by the letter and by this personal attack. Kelly felt much the same, and we both had to pray about it and let it go. It took a great deal of prayer for both of us to get past the issue, and I had to remind myself that this was the birth mother's way of showing us that she was the rightful parent, and that we were not.

It was the third snowfall of the season that third week in January. Snow in our area of the state was rare, and often did not stay on the ground. This snowfall was different, though. School had been out for three days, Monday through Wednesday, as a thick layer of ice coated all of the roads, and cloaked the whole county with its slick beauty. Our own children were in their own personal Heaven, as they fully embraced the type of Snow Day that I enjoyed as a youth in the Northern state of Michigan. Right after breakfast, the three of them sprinted outside and sled down the steep driveway like an Olympic luger athlete, using the sleds my parents had brought down from up north. Soon afterward, I joined them, and showed them that their father was an expert bobsledder. Even Grace joined in on the fun, as she took a couple of rides down the glossy driveway before surrendering to wet socks and chilled fingers.

By Thursday, much of the ice had melted from the landscape, and many of the buses were able to make the trip down the county roads. All along, I had scoffed at the fact that school had been cancelled for what I deemed a tiny amount of snow and ice. Compared to the snow storms that enveloped the state where my parents still lived, I found the cancellation of school where we now lived slightly humorous. The joke was about to be played on me.

The road we lived on was a long dirt one, which stretched for a few miles. That Friday morning, it was covered in ice. Experience had taught me that driving on the road would be no problem, as long as I did it slowly and carefully, as my Michigan training had taught me, a long long time ago, in a state far far away. The day before, Kelly and I had journeyed forth carefully to school and work and then back home safely enough. Why should it be any different on Friday? After all, the ice had melted some over the twenty four hour period. It will be just fine, I told myself. To quote my Aussie wife, "No worries, mate!"

The DeGarmo caravan of two cars headed off to school early that Friday morning, giving us plenty of time to traverse the slick road. Kelly's car was in the front, with our four children, while I drove behind her, taking Micah, Joshua, and Linda to the day care center. The road was a bumpy one, and any car that trekked down it was certain to hit a pot hole every few seconds; it was a rough ride any day of the year. Driving no more than fifteen miles per hour, the car soon started spinning after it came off a pot hole. "Oh, no...," I groaned to myself, as the car headed ever so unhurriedly towards the side embankment. "I can't believe this....," was my next thought, as the car slowly thumped into the embankment and gradually rolled onto its side. The automobile misfortune was so very slow, resulting in no injuries to the four of us. I promptly turned around to check on the children. Strapped in tight into their car seats, all three stared back at me, with looks that ranged from surprised to quizzical to bemused. "Is everyone okay?" I asked, as they hung from the straps of their car seats, legs swinging freely. Micah and Joshua broke into grins, while Linda simply sat there, or perhaps it was that she swung there.

165

After a quick reconnaissance that everyone was safe and quite secure, I unbuckled and climbed out the passenger window. A frantic wave of my arms failed in getting Kelly's attention, as her car continued on down the road.

"Drat, she's gone," I mused. Pulling out her extra cell phone she lent me that morning, I called her other phone. "Kelly, I'm okay," I said, with a dazed smile. "I need you to please come back, as my car flipped over. I'm okay, and the kids are fine, too. No worries. Just come on back when you get a chance. Love you."

Next was the school. "Could you please tell the principal that I shall be momentarily late? I seemed to have flipped my car over," I told the secretary. Another call and the tow truck was on its way, followed by the sheriff's department and local ambulance. It seemed that the whole town was going to turn out. The children were still smiling, as I peered into the car window, standing on my tip toes. I figured I had three options before me. First, drag the children out into the thirteen degree temperature and allow them to quickly freeze. Second, drag the children out and watch them slip and slide all over the road, resulting in potential injury. Third, keep the children strapped into their seats, where they were warm and safe. Taking my harmonica out of my pocket, I chose the third option, and played some songs for them, as well as sang "Jesus loves me," while we waited for help to arrive. Moments later, it did, as a parade of vehicles came; three sheriff patrol cars, an ambulance, the tow truck, Kelly, and some neighbors. After reassuring all that we were fine and sending the ambulance on its way, I pulled the kids out of the car and loaded them into Kelly's car, whereupon she took them to day care. Next, I filled out the police report, while my car was righted. As it was drive able, I headed off to work, myself. God had surely been with me, as I paused to think through much of the day what it might have been like if the three children had been injured.

We were tired, worn out, drained. It felt like I was sleep walking through my days, and Kelly felt the same. Still, when it came time for the children to go back to their mothers, I was not ready to give them up easily.

Their mother had gotten a job at a local fast food restaurant, and in the eyes of DFCS, was now able to appropriately take care of her children. I received this news over the phone by their caseworker, Susan, and immediately I began to protest.

"Susan, when I take foster children into my home, they become my children, and I fight for them as if they were my own. I wonder if this young mother will be able to provide for them all that they need. How can someone who is so young, and by herself, make sure that Micah, who has severe learning disabilities, and Joshua, who has anger issues, get the resources they need to thrive? Kelly and I have struggled enough by ourselves to provide what these children require. How can she, by herself? Besides this, it was less than three months ago that she was beating them with an electrical cord. Are you telling me that because she has a job now, she no longer has these issues?" I was frustrated, and I was concerned. I just didn't want to see these children placed back in an environment where they would take steps backwards, where they would suffer. Worse, I didn't want to see what happened to Sydney happen to these boys. My phone call did nothing to change the situation, though I did feel better knowing that I at least tried. After all, every child needs someone to fight for them.

Five days after the car accident, the two boys and their little sister left our home. We said our goodbyes to each of them, covering them with kisses and hugs, before I dropped them off at the day care, where Susan would pick them up later that afternoon, to be reunited with their mother. For Kelly, it was the hardest, as she grieved the loss of baby Linda. My last request for Susan was that she contact us if the three should come back into care. I prayed for their sake, though, that they wouldn't need us or our help again.

CHAPTER 15

"Boom, Cathy called me earlier this morning…." Kelly said. I could hear her tired smile on the other end of the phone as I sat at my desk at work, ordering books for the next school year. It had only been nine days since Micah, Joshua, and Linda had left us. Immediately, I gave her my full attention; this couldn't be another Call again, could it? "She wants to know if we can take a baby."

My first reaction was to laugh. Perhaps it was a laugh of insanity, perhaps of exhaustion, perhaps something else. "Kelly, it hasn't even been ten days yet."

"I know, and I told Cathy that I'm still not over losing the others."

"Well, what did she tell you?"

"It's an eighteenth month old baby girl, that's all she knew at the moment. She called about an hour ago, and I prayed about it while giving a massage. Cathy did say that there is already a home for the baby, but she wondered if we could take her, as our house is closer to the birth family than the other. The fact that the baby already has a home makes me feel better. I don't think I'm ready for this…"

I was still suffering from the initial surprise. It HAD only been a few days, and I hadn't recovered, as well. Besides, didn't our family need a break from those long four months? "Yeah…I don't know, either. It may be too soon. Let's pray about it. Heavenly Father, we don't know what to do. We want to serve You, and we thank You for the opportunity to care for Micah, Joshua, and Linda. Please give us a sign on what You would want us to do. Amen."

"Amen," Kelly replied. "I don't think I'm ready, Boomie."

"I agree. I'll call Cathy," I answered, before finishing my conversation with Kelly. I then called Cathy, and filled her in on our decision. "I'm sorry. But, please, don't think we are saying no to fostering, we just don't feel that God is calling us to take this baby right now. Besides, Cathy it's not even been ten days yet, and neither of us are over the loss of the others. Maybe in three more days, we might be ready..." I said, trying to lighten the mood. Telling me she understood and appreciated how we felt, she agreed to call us back if another need arose in the future.

The future was only four days later when The Call came again. "Hey, John, It's Cathy from DFCS again. Hope I'm not bothering you."

"No, not at all, Cathy," I was glad to hear her voice, as I felt we let her down a bit earlier in the week. "How can I help you?"

"Well, you told me to wait a few days...," she said before pausing, a nervous laugh escaping her. "...and it has been four days...." It was my turn to laugh, and I let out a hearty one. Then she hit me with a bombshell, "We have a family of five children who need a home, and...."

I nearly fell off my chair, as I burst out, interrupting her. "FIVE CHILDREN?"

"Yes, but only three of them need a home," she quickly responded. The caseworker, who had become very familiar with our family, and a valued friend of ours, went on to detail the situation for me. The family of five children needed a home as their parents both suffered from a Meth addiction, which was rapidly becoming the replacement for Crack. Another family in a nearby town had taken in the two younger girls, a four year old and a four month old. The remaining three were boys, aged six, nine, and three. According to Cathy, DFCS was unsure how long the children might be in custody, but it was likely that it would be long term, as the mother faced time in rehab, as did the father, who also faced a prison sentence. "I know this is a lot, John, and I will sure understand if you say no," Cathy assured me, before allowing me time to discuss it with Kelly.

A quick call to Kelly assured me of what I already felt; we're DeGarmos and we foster, it's what we do, and I told Cathy as much; we would take the boys into our home. At times, I don't want to foster. There are moments when I want to hide from the added responsibilities of having more children in the house; needy children, hurt children, sad children. There are mornings where I wish I could get just a bit more rest, sleepwalking through the days. I was tired of having my heart broken again and again as I watched a child leave my home only to be returned to an environment that was unpleasant, unhealthy, and even hostile.

Yet, there are so many children who need a foster home and so few homes willing to embrace them. Fostering is a call, and God's call on our family is clear. He wants Kelly and I to take up this cross of His and look after His children.

ABOUT THE AUTHOR

Dr. John N. DeGamo wrote his doctoral dissertation on The Challenges that Foster Children Face in Rural Schools. He has written for numerous magazines, and is working on his second book. He is happily married to his Australian wife, and they not only raise four of their own children, but have also had over 25 foster children share their home with them. He currently resides in Monticello, Georgia, where he is employed as a media specialist for two local schools. In his spare time, he enjoys gardening, music, and all things Bela Lugosi.

Made in the USA
Lexington, KY
31 January 2013